Dare
to become a
Man of God

By Mikaela Vincent

---

30 Devotionals from a Mother's Heart to Her Son's on
Drawing Near to Christ and Living Victoriously

Text and cartoons copyright © 2010 by Mikaela Vincent
Current revised version copyright © 2014 by Mikaela Vincent

More than a Conqueror Books
morethanaconquerorbooks@gmail.com
www.morethanaconquerorbooks.com

All Scripture quotations, unless otherwise indicated, are taken from the Holy Bible, New King James Version. Copyright © 1982 by Thomas Nelson, Inc. Used by permission. All rights reserved.
Scripture quotations marked (NIV) are taken from the Holy Bible, New International Version®, NIV®. Copyright © 1973, 1978, 1984 by Biblica, Inc.™ Used by permission of Zondervan. All rights reserved worldwide. www.zondervan.com

Contents

Part I: First Things First
- 1 Dare to Fix Your Eyes on Jesus 9
- 2 Dare to Seek God's Kingdom First 12
- 3 Dare to Be Content 14
- 4 Dare to Know Who You Are in Christ 17
- 5 Dare to Walk in Intimacy with Christ 20

Part II: Diving Deeper
- 6 Dare to Worship 24
- 7 Dare to Pray 26
- 8 Dare to Listen to the Voice that Counts 29
- 9 Dare to Obey the King of Kings 32
- 10 Dare to Fear the Lord 34
- 11 Dare to Be Humble 37

Part III: At War
- 12 Dare to Know the Truth and Live It 41
- 13 Dare to Defy Enemy Schemes 44
- 14 Dare to Fight for the Things that Matter 46
- 15 Dare to Cover Over and Armor Up 49
- 16 Dare to Walk by Faith 52
- 17 Dare to Be Filled with the Spirit 54
- 18 Dare to Shrink Not from Death 56

Part IV: Out There
- 19 Dare to Share Christ with the Lost 60
- 20 Dare to Feed God's Sheep 62
- 21 Dare to Treat Women Right 64
- 22 Dare to Love Your Bride as Christ Loves His 66
- 23 Dare to Care About the Needs of Others 68

Part V: Improving Your Serve
- 24 Dare to Mentor and Be Mentored 71
- 25 Dare to Love 73
- 26 Dare to Forgive 75
- 27 Dare to See with God's Eyes 77
- 28 Dare to Submit to Authority 80
- 29 Dare to Walk in Integrity 82
- 30 Dare to Glorify God in Everything 84

Leader's Guide 87

My dear son,

I smiled as I wrote this for you, because you are already becoming a man of God. Your passion for Him and your heart for the lost and hurting already mark you as His.

God has unique adventures planned just for you. He wants to equip you now to climb the steep faces of every mountain and rappel off every cliff in life with excitement and faith, not fear.

The Word of God is your lifeline.

So hold on tightly to the truth, wrap it around your waist (Ephesians 6:14), and secure it to your heart, until what it says is who you are.

Don't worry if some of the things God is teaching you seem difficult at first. Just keep climbing. He'll show you where the secure footholds are so you won't slip. And if you fall, He is able to catch you.

Most of all, love God with all your heart, and never doubt His fathomless love for you.

I love you always,

Your Mom

To the young men who will read this book:

I'm so glad you're taking this journey with us!

Although I wrote this book for the son I gave birth to, I've written it also for you.

The experiences on these pages relate to our personal life together as a family and may be very different from what you have experienced. You may not have a little sister. You may never have lived overseas. And you may not even have a godly father or mother in your life.

That's okay. This book is still for you.

My hope is that you, like my amazing husband, will be a man of God one day (if you aren't one already!), and the woman you marry will be blessed beyond measure, just as I have been.

Don't be discouraged if some of the qualities of a man of God on these pages seem out of your reach, especially if you never grew up with a good example in your household...

Because they're not!

You have a heavenly Father, and He wants to show you how it's done.

The mistakes that were made before you can stop now with you, if you choose. You can be the one who makes the choice to live as God made you to live, love as He made you to love, and enjoy life to its fullest in Him.

In fact ...

I dare you to become a Man of God!

In His love,

"Momma" Mikaela

Suggestions for how to use this devotional:

Keep a journal. You were created for relationship. So think of this journal as letters written by you to Someone you love, and from your loved One to you. Let Him change the way you see things. And keep looking back at what He's teaching you so you won't forget it, and so you can walk out in those truths. Let Him change your LIFE! You can use a blank notebook with lines in it for a journal; or if you like to draw, you can find one without lines (try the sketch book aisle in an art store).

Look up the scriptures in each chapter. My words don't matter so much. It's His Word that will change you. I like to write in the margins of my Bible the things He is teaching me from each passage. Then, every time I open my Bible to that passage, I'm reminded of what He said, and it makes it easier to walk out in that truth.

Take your time through each chapter. Don't be in a hurry to get through this book. Every chapter has deep jewels in it God wants you to truly learn and walk out in, not just skim through. The daily applications at the end of each chapter are lifestyle-changing, if you let them become a habit rather than something you do just once. You might want to continue using this devotional even after you've completed it, going back through the daily applications so you can get in the habit of doing those things and asking your heart those questions.

Have a daily quiet time. Don't let a day go by without this important time alone with Jesus. Choose a time in the day that is good for you. Everyone's quiet time is different, so don't feel like yours has to look like someone else's or happen at the same time of day as theirs. Feel free to be creative. I like to start my morning with Jesus, just doing whatever He's doing that day: worship, or just listen to Him, or pray, or read the Word, or let Him show me things in my heart He wants to change, or study through a devotional. Then at night, I read the Bible (I like to just read until He shows me something, and then stop, meditate on what He said, and pray it back to Him), so that what He says is the last thing in my mind as I fall asleep.

Get your friends involved. Introduce this devotional to others who will journey with you through it, doing the chapters in their own quiet times, and then talking together with you each week about what God is showing them. You will learn more if you are sharing what you're learning, and hearing what He's teaching others, as well. You might even want to gather together as a group to do this as a weekly Bible study. (See suggestions at the end of the book for how to lead a group Bible study.)

STOP!

BEFORE YOU READ ANY FURTHER,

PRAY!

God, open my eyes to see what You want me to see…

To hear Your voice…

To know You more…

To walk in Your ways…

To become like You…

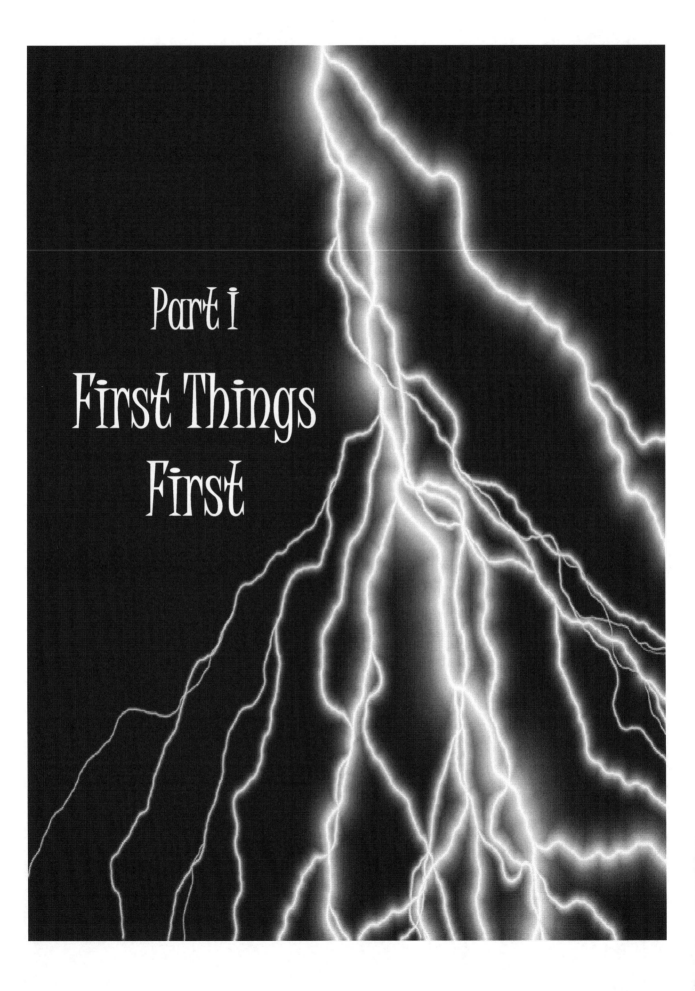

Part I
First Things First

Dare to Fix Your Eyes on Jesus

Run for Your Life!

Imagine you're running a race. You've trained for this. Your plan is to win. The prize is a million dollars.

The weather's perfect—a cloud cover, a slight breeze. The track is level. You're running at a good pace thinking, *"I can do this!"*

But then the sun breaks through the clouds and something sparkles on the track. It looks like... Yes, it must be. You can't believe your luck! You stop, bend down, and pick it up.

A *penny!*

Okay. You're thinking, Mom, that's stupid! I wouldn't do that! I'd lose the race, and miss out on a million dollars!

Yes, you're right. But unfortunately, many runners in the Christian life, which the Word calls a "race," have missed out because something less worthy distracted them.

A good runner must fix his eyes on what he's running for and run undistracted.

A "penny" in this case might be something you want that isn't God's best for you (riches, fame, pornography, sex, video games or movies that take all your time and fill your mind, etc.).

But looking around at the other runners and comparing yourself to them can mislead you, as well. You might think you're doing better than you are, or not well enough.

Running well is something you grow into; as you spend daily times with the Lord and lean on Him in difficult life situations. *Believers who "run" well have developed spiritual "muscles" through "exercise."*

So don't worry if you think you don't run as well as someone else. Just *fix your eyes on Jesus,* and trust His training program to get you where you need to go at just the pace He has for you.

"Let us lay aside every weight, and the sin which so easily ensnares us, and let us run with endurance the race that is set before us, looking unto Jesus, the author and finisher of our faith."
Hebrews 12:1b-2a

Have you ever seen a runner in the Olympics carry an anvil?

Of course not! But wrong thought processes or enemy lies (anything we believe or act out of that is contrary to what God says) can weigh us down. (2 Corinthians 10:3-5. John 8:42-47)

Use a colored pencil or highlighter to highlight here in this book that definition in the parentheses above of a "lie," or copy it into your journal.

Now stop for a moment and consider your own actions and thought processes. Is there anything like that in your life you need to "throw off" in order to run faster? Explain.

_____
_____
_____
_____
_____
_____

Say, for instance, God gives you an amazing leadership opportunity at school, and you can't wait to glorify Him in it. But then a teacher criticizes you and tells you you're doing it all wrong.

"But I thought God gave me this opportunity. I thought He wanted to use me to shine for Him. But it's not really working out that way. So I must have been wrong." Angry at God, you quit.

That's a bit drastic. But can you see how believing something that's not true can deter you from the course God has you on?

What if God leads you to talk about Him with your friends, but you're afraid they won't think you're "cool" anymore if you do? So you let fear of man control you rather than the Holy Spirit.

Hebrews 12 addresses sin as something that ensnares or entangles us—like a runner in baggy pants that sag to his knees. That'll trip you up and land your nose in the dirt for sure! Have you ever felt that way when you've fallen to sin? Explain.

_____
_____
_____
_____
_____

Write the truth below in your journal:

Everyone makes mistakes. The difference for the one who fixes his eyes on Jesus is that he grows through those mistakes and runs all the faster.

1 John 1:9 says: "If we confess our sins, He is faithful and just to forgive us our sins and to cleanse us from all unrighteousness."

Line your race track with that truth, and if ever you do trip and fall, you won't have to worry about the ground opening up to swallow you in a muddy pit of guilt and condemnation. (Romans 8:1)

The key to running unhindered is to fix your eyes on Jesus. If He is your first love, your one passion, then temptations and lies will lose their appeal next to the joy of running toward Him.

This whole journey is about relationship, not works. So, don't just try to will yourself to do the right thing, although your will to follow Christ is most certainly crucial. **Seek to fall deeper in love with Him, then let His love and your passion for Him fuel your will to come in line with His.** (Romans 8:35-39)

Re-read the paragraph above and write in your own words what it says to your heart.

_____
_____
_____
_____
_____
_____
_____
_____

"Everyone who competes for the prize (does) it to obtain a perishable crown, but we for an imperishable crown."
1 Corinthians 9:25

Want to Run Faster?

Close your eyes and picture yourself running the race. Ask God to show you:

What is weighing you down, making it harder to run after Him?

_____
_____
_____
_____

Look at the cartoon on the next page. Which character are you? Is there a burden you need to hand to Him, a worry maybe? Or a fear? Or something from your past? Something you keep holding onto, even though it's slowing you down? If you could describe it as one of those things weighing down the man on the right, which of those would it feel most like? Explain.

_____
_____
_____
_____
_____
_____
_____

Are any sins or lies tripping you up? Explain.

_____
_____

What distracts you? What often takes your eyes off of Jesus?

How do you feel you've run the race in the past?

And how do you want to run it from now on?

In a time of prayer right now, picture yourself taking off those burdens, sins, and thoughts that hinder you, and handing them to Jesus. Write a prayer to Him from your heart, handing Him those things. Picture Him taking them from you, freeing you to run to Him at high speed. Now, *fix your eyes on Jesus, knowing HE is your Prize.*

Get in the habit of daily (and even all throughout the day) cleaning out your heart and mind before the Lord, throwing off everything that hinders you, so you can run fast, strong, and with JOY in this race of life.

Dare to Seek God's Kingdom First

What Do You Want Most?

If a genie gave you three wishes, what would you wish for?

1. _____
2. _____
3. _____

Would those things really be enough to make you happy for the rest of your life?

The truth is, no matter how much you run after the things you want or need in life, those things will never satisfy you. Only a deep, intimate relationship with Christ will.

Why? Because it is what you were created for.

No one on this earth gets to live a problem-free life. But we can live a joy-filled life, if we tap into the right Source.

The key to contentment is found in Psalm 87:7:

"All my springs are in you."

If you know Who the Source of your joy is, then you will never wander far, for your thirst will drive you back to Him.

That's how Paul could say in Philippians 4:12-13 (NIV),

"I know what it is to be in need, and I know what it is to have plenty. I have learned the secret of being content in any and every situation, whether well fed or hungry, whether living in plenty or in want. I can do everything through Him who gives me strength."

What does Matthew 6:25-34 mean to you?

_____
_____
_____

When God created you, it was for this purpose: *to know Him and enjoy Him and bring Him glory.*

God Almighty made you because He loves you. That's good news, because that means…

Seeking God first positions you for the BEST things in life.

"But seek first the kingdom of God and His righteousness, and all these things shall be added to you." Matthew 6:33

When I was in college, the "perfect man" asked me to marry him. He was charming, handsome, and rich. He even taught Bible study at his church. He seemed everything a girl would want in a husband. But I said no because I didn't feel my God saying yes.

And I'm so glad! Later, God brought your father into my life, and no earthly mansion the other man offered me could compare to the incredible adventures we have experienced carrying the good news to the ends of the earth and having you for a son.

Surrendering to God is to your advantage.

If you are truly seeking God's will, you are not likely to miss it. How do I know that? Because Jeremiah 29:13 says,

"You will seek Me and find Me, when you search for Me with all your heart."

It's a promise you can count on!

But what if your heart confuses you, and you want something so badly, you think God wants it for you too? What if you make a colossal mistakes you regret for the rest of your life?

God is STILL in control. His purposes for you still stand: **to know Him and enjoy Him and bring Him glory.**

Nothing surprises God; not even the messes we make. He knows what we're going to do long before we do it. And He already has a plan to use everything for good. (Romans 8:28)

God is bigger than our messes.

A cool car, a good career, and a beautiful wife are all things that can "break down" at some point, even when you're following God. But He turns every difficulty into a chance to draw closer to Him.

Look for what God has for you instead of what you think you want for yourself, and you will find He is all you need.

If God is your First Love, then His desires become your desires, and any other blessings are just a bow on the gift of Himself.

"For me, to live is Christ…" Philippians 1:21a

No one gets everything he wants in this world, except the man whose desire is for God. Then God will most certainly satisfy him with Himself.

"Delight yourself also in the Lord, and he shall give you the desires of your heart." Psalm 37:4

Want the Best for Your Life?

Is there anything you worry about? Good grades? Finding the right wife? Choosing a career? Which university to attend? Knowing God's will and purpose for your life? Explain.

_____
_____

What are some things you are hoping to have in your future?

_____
_____
_____
_____
_____

God already has a perfect plan for your life. The Sovereign One who created you, who loves you with no boundaries, has already planned for you the BEST…

HIMSELF!

What does Jeremiah 29:11-13 say about God's plans for His people?

_____
_____
_____
_____
_____

Write a prayer, handing your future over to Him, knowing that as you obey Him and trust in Him, He will give you more of Himself. And ***He makes everything in life taste better!***

_____
_____
_____
_____
_____
_____
_____
_____

Get in the habit of laying all your plans before the Lord, so that you only do whatever He is doing. (John 5:19) Let Him be the One you want more than anything else in life, so He can lovingly guide your future according to His plan, filling it with His joy, peace, and blessing, even through the hard times.

Dare to Be Content

3

Genies Aside...

Write about a time when you expected or hoped something would happen, but it didn't. How did that make you feel?

_____
_____
_____
_____
_____
_____

What if you hope for a great job making lots of money and then find yourself delivering pizzas instead?

I actually have a friend who felt called by God to deliver pizzas for a season of his life. With four children, it was difficult to make ends meet, but he became a light in the darkness. He met the home-alone kids, the lonely, the hurting. He blessed them with words and love. At the end of the day, he took leftover pizzas to feed the homeless. Because his family had to live in a poor neighborhood, they too had the opportunity to share Christ daily with the needy and hurting.

Read 1 Timothy 6:6-11. How can desire for money be dangerous?

_____
_____
_____

What should you pursue instead?

_____
_____

This is not to say you shouldn't work hard and do well in life. God may call you to be a successful businessman and live in a mansion. All I'm saying is: **The job you have and how many things you have should not be the source of your joy.**

The only treasures that last are the eternal ones—like intimacy with Christ, faith, love, salvation, joy, peace, eternal security, etc.

"Do not lay up for yourselves treasures on earth, where moth and rust destroy and where thieves break in and steal; but lay up for yourselves treasures in heaven, where neither moth nor rust destroys and where thieves do not break in and steal. For where your treasure is, there your heart will be also." Matthew 6:19-21

Grab hold of the freedom and joy of knowing that *the God who loves you is in control*. He knows your past, He knows your future, and He knows what you're going through now.

He has a plan, and it's a good one. (Romans 8:28) He *LOVES* you. And that's a peaceful place to rest.

With God, even the hard things can be turned into joy and fulfillment.

Read Hosea 2:14-23. God led the Israelites into a desert, a Valley of "Trouble" (Achor). As He spoke tenderly through their hard times, that Valley of Trouble became a door of _____. (v. 15)

Their view of God was transformed through those hard times. They stopped calling Him "Master" (Baal), and called Him _____. (v. 16)

What does that mean to you?

_____
_____
_____
_____
_____

Life's deserts bubble with refreshing springs when we lean on the One we love. (Psalm 42, Song of Songs 8:5)

Read Deuteronomy 32:10-11. What else does God do with us in the desert?

_____
_____
_____

The word in Hebrew for "shield" also means to "surround" and to "change direction."

If you look to the Lord, the One who loves you, surrounds you, and shields you in the hard times—rather than looking at how bad your circumstances are—that "desert" place can become a life-changing experience.

There is one more key to contentment:

A THANKFUL HEART.

If you thank God and worship Him, even in the hard times, you will be "content" no matter what. (Philippians 4:11-13)

Thanking God changes your viewpoint from looking at the dark side to seeing what He's done and has yet to do.

One time, when you and your sister were babies, your father became so ill he could have died. At the same time, you two were sick with diarrhea

and vomiting. It felt like such a battle, and yet, I was so busy washing and changing all of your clothes and sheets, trying to keep all of you hydrated with liquids so you wouldn't die, and comforting you and holding you every time you cried, that I had no time to sleep, much less to fight the battle the way it needed to be fought: *in prayer.*

I was worried, harried, exhausted, sleep-deprived, and at my wits' end. But as I cleaned up and held all of you in turn, I began just thanking God for the gift each of your lives has been to me, and for all the other beautiful things God has done, like giving His Son to die for us, providing a roof over our heads and food to eat.... I even thanked Him for His healing before He healed you.

Not only did He heal all three of you, but **He changed my anxious heart into a peaceful one.** And **I learned just how powerful the strategy of thanking God is against our enemy!**

> "Rejoice in the Lord always. Again I will say, rejoice! Let your gentleness be known to all men. The Lord is at hand. **Be anxious for nothing**, but in everything by prayer and supplication, with **thanksgiving**, let your requests be made known to God; and the **peace** of God, which surpasses all understanding, will guard your hearts and minds through Christ Jesus."
>
> Philippians 4: 4-7

Want Peace?

Is there something you want that you don't have? Write about it here.

_____
_____
_____
_____

What troubles are you facing?

_____
_____
_____
_____
_____

Hand those things over to God, and spend some time thanking Him and praising Him. Write your prayer to Him here.

_____
_____
_____
_____
_____
_____
_____
_____
_____
_____
_____
_____
_____

Now, ask Him what He thinks about the things you need or want. Listen to what He might speak to your heart or show you in His Word, and write what comes to mind.

_____
_____
_____
_____
_____
_____
_____
_____
_____
_____
_____
_____

Don't worry if you can't hear Him clearly yet. Just keep asking Him and looking for His answer. If you continue to love Him, obey Him, talk with Him, and listen for His voice, He won't let you miss what He's doing in your life.

Get in the habit of thanking God, and handing everything over to Him, resting in his Sovereignty. (Isaiah 30:15) Surrender to Him, knowing you can trust Him, even if the outcome isn't what you expected, because He is GOOD.

Dare to Know Who You Are in Christ

4

Wear the Right Hat!

Did you know that when you chose to follow Christ, your identity changed?

"You are no longer a slave but a son, and if a son, then an heir of God through Christ."
Galatians 4:7

Wow! From a slave to a prince and heir to a kingdom! That just doesn't happen on this earth. But God's kingdom operates by different standards. (1 Corinthians 1:26-31)

"He who is joined to the Lord is one spirit with Him." 1 Corinthians 6:17

Belonging to the Kingdom of God means a change in your loyalties. (2 Corinthians 5:17)

In other words, you no longer do things because the people you hang out with do it that way. Nor do you do things according to the culture you grew up in or live in.

You're an "alien" now.

Not the kind with spindly arms, green skin, and antennas! That's just in the movies.

But you are extra-terrestrial in a sense. Heaven is your home now. (1 Peter 1:17; 2:11-12)

That means…

You do things the way Jesus does, not the way others think you should.

Let's hash this out. Say you're the leader of a team, and one person is not keeping up with the workload. Do you…

    a. Talk about it, but not to him?

    b. Compare him to someone else to shame him into doing the right thing?

    c. Talk around the subject to him, hoping he guesses the meaning?

    d. Get someone else to talk to him?

    e. Speak harshly and threaten him to scare him into working harder?

    f. Confront him in front of others?

Each of these is actually protocol in certain cultures of the world. Even in the same country, cultures vary from north to south, or even family to family.

A guy could wear himself out trying to dance to so many tunes!

What does Galatians 1:10 say?

_____
_____
_____

The truth is **only God's opinion really matters. And you please Him already just because you're His son.** Now that's a freeing thought!

So, take every piece of advice to Him, and measure it with His Word and His heart of love (Matthew 22:37-40) before you receive it.

Okay. So let's look back at that situation with the slacker. What would you do as the leader in that situation?

_____
_____
_____
_____

What would Jesus do? (See Matthew 18:15, Ephesians 4:15, and Mark 10:35-45.)

_____

_____
_____
_____

The world makes decisions based on what others expect of them, or what seems best, or personal gain, or fear, or low self-esteem, or any number of thoughts, urges, or emotions.

But you are a prince, an heir to God's kingdom.

You make decisions based on Christ's lordship over your life.

Your boss may urge you to do something acceptable in the business world. But if it is against your King's instructions, graciously decline. Even if you lose much by worldly standards, it's worth it for the heavenly rewards. (2 Corinthians 4:17-18. Philippians 3:7-8)

What are some things in the culture you're living in right now that clash with Kingdom of Heaven culture? (dating practices? ungodly holidays? What else?)
_____
_____
_____
_____

Satan loves to use experiences in life and other people to tell you who you are. But if it doesn't line up with what God and His Word say, it's just a plain old lie. (John 8:43-47)

So throw Romans 8:37 in Satan's face next time you feel like a failure.

Stick him with 1 Corinthians 1:26-30 whenever he tells you you're nothing or you're stupid.

Stand on Hebrews 10:14 and Romans 8:1 whenever you feel you don't measure up.

Declare Philippians 4:13 next time you feel you can't do anything right.

In fact, in the following two columns below, under "LIES," write the above common lies Satan likes to tell God's people ("I'm a failure," "I don't measure up," "I'm worthless," "I can't do anything right"). Then look up the verses mentioned above, and write what God's truth is in the "Truth" column next to the lie His Word demolishes.

LIES	TRUTH
_____	_____
_____	_____
_____	_____
_____	_____
_____	_____
_____	_____
_____	_____
_____	_____
_____	_____
_____	_____
_____	_____
_____	_____
_____	_____
_____	_____

Have you ever believed any of those lies about yourself? Explain.
_____
_____
_____
_____

Ask God what other lies you might believe. John 8:42-47. Begin by reminding yourself of the last time you reacted negatively to something someone said or did. Ask God why you felt that way. Look for lies like, "I have to defend myself," or "I'm all alone," or "No one gets me," or "I need it," or any other sentences that come up as your reason for reacting. Write here what comes to mind.
_____
_____
_____
_____
_____

Now, ask God for His truth to knock them down. If you don't know what scriptures hold the truth, try looking up a word in a concordance (there are some good ones on line) that means the opposite of what you feel. For instance, if you feel anxious, look up "peace" or "faith."

> ***Most people receive their identity through what they do, but your identity is found in what Christ has done for you.***
>
> ***You are who HE says you are, not what others say you are.***

Want to Be Real?

What do these verses say about your identity in Christ?

John 15:15: I am *Jesus' friend* _____

1 Corinthians 6:19: I am _____

1 Corinthians 12:27: I am _____

Hebrews 10:14: I am _____

Galatians 5:13: I am _____

Psalm 103:12: I am _____

Ephesians 2:10: I am _____

1 Corinthians 3:9: I am _____

Acts 1:8: I am _____

Matthew 5:14: I am _____

2 Corinthians 5:20: I am _____

Ephesians 2:19: I am _____

Get in the habit of walking out in the truth of who you are in Christ. If you are Jesus' friend, then talk with Him, hang out with Him, know He's with you everywhere you go, and that He is FOR you. If you are His Son, then take on His qualities, His morals, His values, His way of speaking and acting, until you look like Him so much, people will know who your Daddy is.

Dare to Walk in Intimacy with Christ

5

Higher Up and Deeper In

Life can be a bit of a bungee jump sometimes, don't you think? Have you ever felt like you were plummeting off a cliff head first into some terrible situation?

There *is* a way to bounce back without dashing on the rocks.

You see, with God, a problem is not a problem. It is an opportunity.

By placing your faith in the "cords" of God's love (Hosea 11:3-4), difficult situations transform into thrilling ones, and your relationship with Christ tightens.

I've been through some tough things in life, but I wouldn't trade them for anything!

I've come to find the more difficult the trial, the more spectacular Jesus is, and the more I fall in love with Him.

In fact, those hard times have been the very things He has used to set me free from whatever heart issues might have made the difficulties in the first place.

But to go through battles in life as "more than a conqueror" (Romans 8:37), you need to tighten the "cord" around you—*your relationship with Christ.*

If you don't, you'll end up like so many Christians who dash upon the same rocks over and over, because they didn't dive into God the first time. They waste every thrilling opportunity for higher heights and deeper depths by getting angry with Him, hiding from Him, or blaming others for their sin and wrong choices. (Ouch! That hurts!) Have you ever done that before? _____

So, how do you tighten that cord?

"Draw near to God, and He will draw near to you." James 4:8.

John 15:1-17 talks about being God's friend. That means sharing the secrets of your heart with Him, even as He shares His with you. (1 Corinthians 4:1)

You see, you were made for relationship with the God who loves you and formed you for Himself. He created you to enjoy His love and love Him back.

The secret to intimacy is a passionate love for God.

"I am in My Father, and you in Me, and I in you. He who has My commandments and keeps them, it is he who loves Me. And he who loves Me will be loved by My Father, and I will love him and manifest Myself to him." John 14:20-21

When you fall in love, you can't stop thinking about the one you love. You long for her, want to be near her, to hear her voice. You find yourself loving the things she loves, taking on opinions and ideas she feels passionately about…

That's what it means to have a passion for God. You want to be one with Him (John 15-17), to know Him so deeply and so well that you take on His viewpoints, His interests, His heart. He's with you all the time, so your conversations never end.

Nothing else matters in life but Him.

He is your first thought when you wake: "Lord, what do you have for me today?"… your last thought as you sleep: "Lord, talk to me in my dreams."... and all your thoughts in between: "Lord, this is hard. Help me, please… Lord, give me the words to speak to this person about You… Lord, what a beautiful sunset You made."

A tree with a taproot of passion for God will dig down deep to draw life from the rivers of His love and produce spiritual fruit aplenty.

In the illustration below right, write "passion for God" on the tap root, and "River of God" on the river. Now read Galatians 5:22-23, and label all the fruit on the tree.

Which of these fruits do you enjoy plenty of?

_____
_____
_____
_____

Which of these do you want more of?

_____
_____
_____
_____

The closer you walk with Christ, the more abundant and meaningful your life will be.
(John 10:10b)

When you and your sister were babies, I lived in continual exhaustion. In fact, nearly every day when I put you two down for your naps, I fell asleep. I didn't mean to, because I was hungry for God, and it was my only time to be alone with Him. But I just couldn't help it.

That longing in my heart to be with Him acted as a magnet, and He came close to me, even as I slept. Often, He would awaken me with dreams of how much He loves me.

But one time, I actually heard His voice audibly. He said, "Come!"

I awoke with a start, not believing it was for real. But twice more He called out to me, "Come. Come!"

More than all the high callings of all the saints,

Jesus calls us first to Himself.

I don't know about you, but I would think that if God were to speak audibly to me, He'd probably boom in some deep voice something like, "I'm calling you to the so-and-so people of such-and-such dark place to preach My good news…"

But no. He called me into my **quiet time.** He called me into His presence, just to be with Him!

So how important is intimacy with Christ? ***It is what you were created for!***

But what if you don't feel a passion for God? What if you don't hunger for Him?

Do you want to? Because that's a great place to start! Tell Him you hunger to hunger for Him, and take steps, like the ones in the following bulleted list, to draw near.

It's not as if He's going anywhere. He's been here next to you all along, waiting for you to notice.

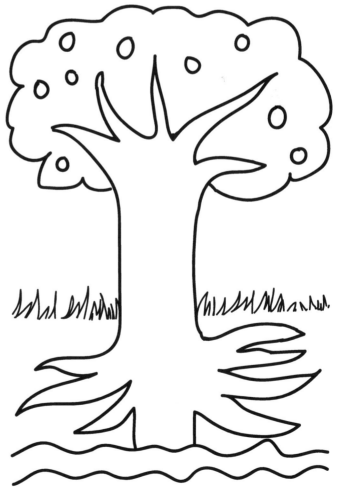

Want to Draw Nearer?

Here are some ways to draw near to God and invite His touch.

- Worship
- Daily quiet times with God
- Prayer
- Listening to God
- Obedience
- Repentance
- Forgiving others
- Loving others
- Surrender
- Humility
- A thankful heart
- Knowing His Word
- Walking in Truth
- Hanging around others who are deep in the Lord
- Teaching others about God

On the roots of the tree to the left, write the points above that you feel are the most crucial to going deep in Christ. Write the others up the trunk of the tree.

Which of the above things do you do often or fell you do well? Why?

_____
_____
_____
_____
_____

Which do you need to do more of? Why?

_____
_____
_____
_____
_____

How will you begin today doing more of those things that will draw you closer to Christ?

_____
_____
_____
_____
_____

Today, look for Jesus as you go about your day. Talk with Him through each situation you face. Ask Him what He's doing so you can walk "in step" with Him. (Galatians 5:25)

Remember, ***if you draw near to God, He will draw near to you.*** (James 4:8)

At the end of the day, journal or write here how this day was different than yesterday. Could you feel His presence more? Did He show you something you might not have noticed if you hadn't been talking with Him throughout the day?

_____
_____
_____
_____
_____
_____

Tomorrow when you wake, make Jesus your first thought. Hand Him your day, and ask Him what He wants to do with it.

Get in the habit of handing Jesus every day before it even starts, and looking for Him throughout the day. As you walk through each situation, share with Him your thoughts, and listen and look for His answers. You are not alone. He wants to do so much in you and through you and all around you, but most of all, with you, *TOGETHER*. Walk in the intimacy with Christ you were created for, and every moment of your life will be a God-moment, pulsating with purpose, meaning, and JOY.

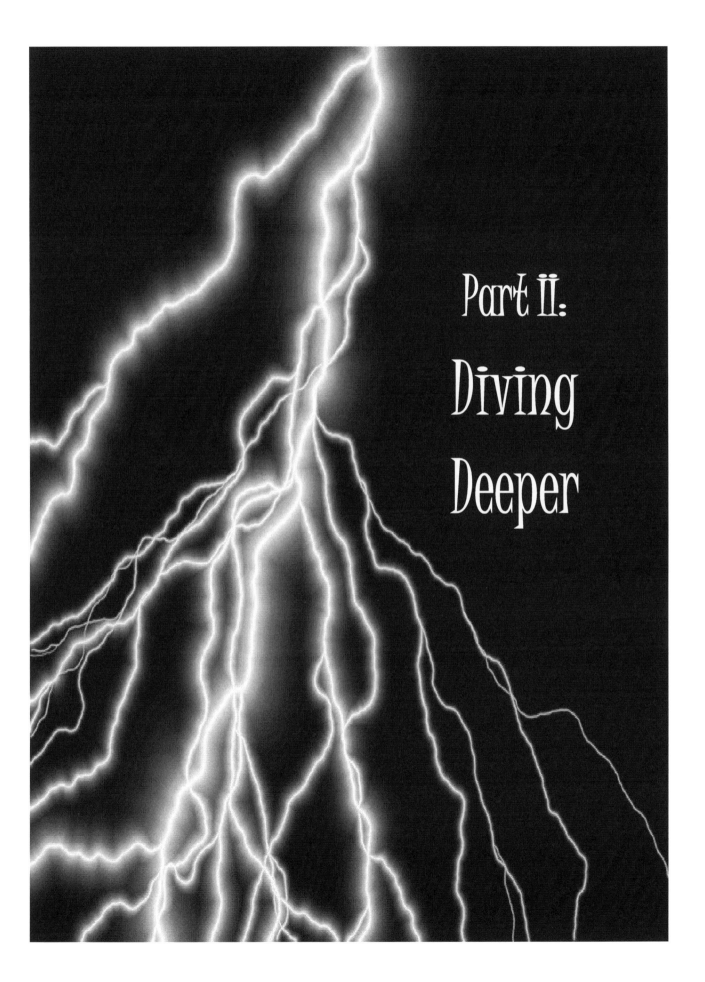

Part II: Diving Deeper

Dare to Worship

The Power of Praise

What are some of God's many names that make Him worthy of worship?

1 Peter 4:19 _____

Deuteronomy 33:27 _____

Jeremiah 16:19 _____
_____
_____

Isaiah 54:5 _____
_____
_____
_____
_____

Genesis 16:13 _____

Exodus 15:26b _____

Other _____
_____

Take a moment to think about God in light of the above. How has He personally demonstrated to you one or more aspects of His character?
_____
_____
_____

Miraculous displays of God's glory are all around us all the time if we would but look for Him.
(Matthew 16:1-4)

But sometimes we get so caught up in what we want or how big our problem is that *we forget how big our God is.* Has that ever happened to you?
_____
_____
_____

Worship ushers in God's felt presence. It invites Him near, and it opens up our hearts to see Him more clearly as He truly is.
(2 Chronicles 6-7)

Have you ever worshipped God and felt His presence near? What was that like? Did He show you something new you hadn't thought about before, or change your mindset about something?
_____
_____
_____
_____
_____
_____

Worship changes you.

Nearly every one of David's psalms that begins with how terrible his predicament is ends with how great his God is.

Try it sometime. Next time you're not sure what to do about a sticky situation, or you feel upset, anxious, discouraged, or angry, spend an hour singing to God or telling Him how amazing He is. You will find your worries fade away in the light of His glory, and He just might meet you in deep, intimate ways, solve your problem for you, or give you direction.

But whether you feel God's touch when you worship or not, whether you feel that He hears your cries for help or not, ***God is still worthy of worship.***
(Job 1:13-20; 13:15; Habakkuk 3:17-18)

So, worship Him.

Do you remember when you were a little boy and you had nightmares or saw things in the night? Whenever you sang praise songs to God, the evil disappeared. That's because…

Worship is a winning strategy against the enemy.

What do these verses tell you about the power of worship: Isaiah 30:32; 2 Chronicles 20:21-22; Exodus 23:25-27; 1 Samuel 16:23?

_____
_____
_____

When God's people worship, Satan's plans are defeated; he is no match for the God of the universe. Not by a long shot. In fact, Satan himself must bow to the King of Kings.

David knew the power of worship as warfare. (Psalm 18) But this man after God's own heart didn't just worship in song; *he worshipped with his life.* (Acts 13:22)

Worship is a lifestyle.

Picture worship in the shape of a cross. The vertical beam is you bringing God glory through praising Him in your quiet times or with others. The horizontal beam is you bringing God glory as you walk out your faith into daily life, living each moment for Him:

Want Meaning in Your Life?

Read the verses below and answer the questions:

*"Oh come, let us sing to the LORD! Let us **shout** joyfully to the Rock of our salvation. Let us come before His presence with **thanksgiving**; Let us shout joyfully to Him with **psalms**. For the LORD is the great God, And the great King above all gods. In His hand are the deep places of the earth; The heights of the hills are His also. The sea is His, for He made it; And His hands formed the dry land. Oh come, let us worship and **bow down**; Let us **kneel** before the LORD our Maker. For He is our God, And we are the people of His pasture, And the sheep of His hand."* Psalm 95:1-7

What are some ways to worship God? Start with the bold lettered words above. But it doesn't end there. Art, dance, writing, declaring...

_____
_____
_____

How do you like to worship God?

_____
_____
_____

Why do we worship Him? See italics in the verses above, and add your own reasons.

_____
_____

What are some ways you can worship God with your lifestyle (how you live your life)?

_____
_____
_____

Spend some time in your quiet time today worshipping God. Write Him a poem, a letter, a song; paint Him a picture, lie prostrate before Him, dance—however He leads. Then, walk out of that worship time purposing to live each moment as if bowed at His feet.

Get in the habit of worshipping God in your quiet times, and in your mind and heart as you walk through your days. Make worship a lifestyle. Live every moment as if bowed at His feet, and your life will be filled with power and purpose.

Dare to Pray

A Friend in High Places

Imagine a thief stalks you. He is seven feet tall. Thick armor covers his bulging muscles. Strapped to his body are daggers, guns, clubs, throwing stars, maces, and nun chucks. His intent is to destroy you.

But the situation isn't hopeless. In fact, you're well connected. With just one punch of a call button, a whole army will join you to fight against him.

"That's nice," you say, as you put the call button on a shelf in the closet.

The thief blasts through the walls of your house in a surprise attack. You head for the closet, but he grabs you by the heels and drags you down, beating you to a pulp with his club. You try to defend yourself, but you're just too weak. In the end he carries away all the things you love most, leaving you in a heap on the floor.

Don't you wish you had kept that call button closer?

We believers have a vicious thief after us (John 10:10), but our connection with the King of Kings ensures we will be more than conquerors. (Romans 8) *Prayer is our call button*, so, as you can imagine…

Your enemy's main aim is to stop you from praying.

He might club you with busyness, or others ridiculing you, or anger at God, or dry quiet times, or self-pity, or sin, or distractions, or fear, or lies. But whatever his methods,

Prayerlessness kills intimacy with Christ. *It will make you powerless to walk in the "better" things.*

Prayer is powerful.

When you were a child growing up in a spiritually dark country, our normal bedtime prayers went something like this: "Jesus, please fill our home with Your presence, and surround it with Your angels. Guard us and all our things from any harm."

When a local business moved in next door, we noticed they parked their bikes in our carport instead of theirs. Finally, your father asked them why. They answered, "Because when we park them in ours, they get stolen, but when we park them in yours, they don't."

"Whatever things you ask in prayer, believing, you will receive." Matthew 21:22

Prayer unites.

- It unites us *with God and His purposes.*
- It unites us *with those who pray with us.*
- It unites us *with those we pray for.*

Imagine with me for a moment that you are a soldier in an army, and enemy archers are raising their bows to shoot at you.

Do you scatter, leaving each man to fend for himself? You could. Maybe your shield would keep you safe for a while.

But what if your army banded together, say, in two rows? The front row kneels, holding out their shields in front. The back row kneels, holding their shields overhead. Each shield interlocks with the other as you face your enemy together, shoulder to shoulder.

The arrows fly, but meet only shield. All your bodies are safely hidden beneath each other's faith as you band together in prayer!

Prayer builds intimacy in relationships and

binds us together in Christ as one with Him.

Prayer releases the power of God upon the earth. *(Revelation 5:8; 8:3-5)*

God is God, and He can do anything He wants any time. But because of His love for us and His design for us to walk in intimate relationship with Him, He most often waits for us to pray before He acts.

He doesn't just want to get something done; He wants to do something with us and in us.

Prayer arms us to win. *(Ephesians 6:10-20)*

Perhaps you find yourself in a room with a particularly annoying person. The enemy would love you to avoid the guy, reject him, and maybe even say something cutting to him. But if you pray, God might lead you instead to show him His love. That love just might even change him!

Prayer tunes us in to what God is doing, so we do what HE leads us to do, *not what the enemy wants.*

Say you're hanging out with your friends and they decide to look at pornography. You could pray and let God show you the "way of escape." (2 Corinthians 10:13) He might give you strength to stand up and walk out the door, or to do or say something to help your friends stand strong against temptation as well. (2 Timothy 2:25-26)

Prayer positions us to see things God's way.

When we pray, we acknowledge that God is Sovereign and we trust Him. We position ourselves to

- submit to His ways
- humble ourselves before Him
- surrender
- see our sin clearly, repent, and be free
- lay down our opinions to pick up His
- defeat the enemy's plans.

In fact, *whenever we pray God's will, the enemy loses ground, and we get closer to God.*

Want Power?

What does the verse below say to your heart?

"Pray in the Spirit on all occasions with all kinds of prayers and requests. With this in mind, be alert, and always keep on praying..."
Ephesians 6:18

_____
_____
_____

Is anything keeping you from praying? Explain.

_____
_____
_____

What will you do to change that?

_____
_____
_____
_____

In your quiet time with the Lord today, write down what you pray for in the left-hand column marked "Prayer Requests" below, and what you feel Him saying to your heart about that request.

Leave the right column open for now, but later (tomorrow or in a few days or months...), come back to this place and write in how God answered your prayer.

What does John 15:7 say about how or why God answers our prayers?

_____
_____
_____

Because of that verse, His answer is usually "yes." especially if you are walking in His Spirit such that your desires are aligned with His desires.

But sometimes His answer is "no," or "not yet." If that is the answer He has given you, feel free to write that in the column to the right, or to change your request on the left, as He leads, to match His desires.

Prayer Requests	Answers
_____	_____
_____	_____
_____	_____
_____	_____
_____	_____
_____	_____
_____	_____
_____	_____
_____	_____
_____	_____
_____	_____
_____	_____

Get in the habit of praying before you make decisions, as you walk into different situations, and even as you speak to others. "Lord, what do YOU want to say? Speak through me... Lord, thank you for the rain today... Lord, what do You want to do now? I want to go there with You..."

Pray without ceasing... In fact, make your life a prayer to Him.

Dare to Listen to the Voice that Counts 8

Tuning In to God

Don't fall into the trap of seeing God as one of those toy machines—work the prayer "crane" just right and you get the toy.

Prayer is a two-way conversation.

When you share with God your needs, listen for His answers and His lessons.

God's voice shakes things up. *(Psalm 29)*

When I'm upset, I tell God how I feel, and then just let His truth wash over me, knocking down any lies, and showing me how He sees things. By the time I walk out of my quiet time, my discouragement or sadness or whatever is turned to *joy* and *peace*.

God's voice changes your perspective.

In fact, keeping a journal of what He says to you will help you not forget it. You can look back on it, and re-seal His words in your heart, making it easier to walk out in those truths every day, as you see things through His eyes and do things His way.

God is talking all the time.

God speaks through

- the Word (2 Timothy 3:16-17)
- circumstances (2 Corinthians 12:7-10; Psalm 40:1-3)
- others (1 Corinthians 2:4-13)
- His still small voice in your mind and heart (Psalm 42:8)
- dreams and visions (Acts 2:17)
- impressions or urgings (Acts 15:28),
- a sense of peace (Philippians 4:7)
- signs and wonders (Acts 2:17-21)
- nature (Psalm 125; 19:1-4)
- and more!

Look back over that list. What is the most common way God speaks to you?

_____
_____
_____
_____

Which ways would you like Him to speak to you more through?

_____
_____
_____
_____
_____

Do you sometimes feel like He's silent? Why?

_____
_____
_____
_____
_____

God speaks even through silence.

If you feel God isn't speaking to you, check and make sure it's not because you're not listening. Are you reading the Word? Setting aside time to be still before Him? Do other things distract you? Have you tried turning distracting thoughts into prayers, and then listening for His answers? Write what you feel blocks you from hearing His voice.

_____
_____
_____
_____
_____

Tuning out God's voice when He speaks is like slamming a door in His face.

29

Have you ever dismissed God's voice with these door slammers: "I just have a wild imagination," or "That's just me," or "I'll think about that later"?

Unconfessed sin (like doubt, worry, pride, self-pity, unforgiveness, etc.) can also block your spiritual ears. Check out your heart before the Lord, and ask Him to forgive you and free you from any sin barriers. Write your prayer here.

_____
_____
_____
_____
_____

Keep the door of your heart open to God. Listen for His voice constantly, and ask Him to help you remove anything in the way between you. Expect Him to answer your prayers and your questions.

*If you expect God to speak,
you are more likely to hear Him.*

What if you think God's speaking, but you're not sure?

Ask Him, "Lord, are you saying such-and-such?" He might confirm it by highlighting a Scripture or sending you a phone call from someone who has been praying for you, or some other way.

If you're still not sure, hand it to Him again: "Lord, it feels like You're saying thus-and-so. I'm going to head that way because I want to obey you. Please make Your will clear."

Even people who walk closely with God can misunderstand Him sometimes. Selfishness, pride, judgment, experience, or any number of other things can get in the way.

But if you run it through this three-fold sieve, and it holds, then it is probably from God:

HOW TO KNOW GOD IS SPEAKING:

1. **Does it line up with the Word (all of it, not just one verse)?**

2. **Does it line up with God's character (especially His love and grace)?**

3. **Does it draw you (and others) closer to Him?**

*The key to listening is **obedience**. Every time you step out in faith to do what He asks of you, **His voice gets louder**.*

But if you ignore Him, there may come a time when you no longer hear Him. (Isaiah 55:6)

When I was thirteen, the Lord spoke through His creation to me. Out under the stars one night, I pointed to a dim one and said, "I feel like that. Everyone around me shines so brightly for You, and I'm barely a twinkle."

A cloud passed over, and the star disappeared. I cried, "Lord, when a cloud of sadness passes over me, no one can see Your light in me at all. I don't want to be like that anymore. I want to shine for You all the days of my life."

The cloud moved, and the star miraculously grew brighter and brighter until it was one of the brightest stars in the sky!

His promise that night filled me with new joy and passion for Him. Suddenly, I was able to shine for Him, no matter how dark the circumstances.

As I shared that testimony with others, however, time and time again missionaries and other people I respected highly in the Lord said to me, "God doesn't speak that way. You were mistaken."

Eventually, after enough people responded that way and no one around me seemed to have experienced Him as I had, I believed them, and closed the door on God's voice.

Twenty years later, He busted down that door. But I had wasted all those years in-between.

Now I listen to God, not man.

"Behold, I stand at the door and knock. If anyone hears My voice and opens the door, I will come in to him and dine with him, and he with Me." Revelation 3:20

Need Hearing Aids?

What do you feel God saying to you through Isaiah 50:4-5 and John 10:1-5?

_____
_____
_____

Take time in your quiet time today to block out every thought or distraction and listen for His voice. (Psalm 46:10) Ask Him a question, or just be still before Him. Write in your journal what you feel Him saying. Then run it through the "three-fold sieve":

1. Does it line up with the Word (all of it)? Why or why not? _____
_____
_____

2. Does it line up with God's character (especially His love)? Why or why not? _____
_____
_____

3. Does it draw you closer to God? Why or why not? _____
_____
_____

Tomorrow morning, as you wake, ask God to give you a word for the day. It might come from a scripture, or you might just feel Him saying something to your heart. Then watch throughout the day with anticipation for Him to do that.

Get in the habit of not only talking to God, but listening for His voice, looking for His answers to your prayers. Don't just do something because you want to; ask God to show you what HE's doing, and let His Spirit flow through you. Tune your spiritual ears in to His voice every moment, even if it seems He's not speaking. He's always speaking. It just might not be the way you expect Him to. If you tune Him out, you'll miss the God-thing that could have made all the difference in your life.

Dare to Obey the King of Kings

9

The Path to Joy and Freedom

What does James 1:22-25 say to your heart?

_____
_____
_____

What about 1 John 5:3-6?

_____
_____

Could you imagine what your life would be like had your father and I not obeyed God? You might not even exist!

We might never have married. We might not have moved to the countries where you have lived. Imagine your life without the amazing experiences God has given you and the depths of His Word and His love that you have known. (Matthew 7:24-27)

Obedience to Christ brings joy, peace, freedom, and blessings. *(Psalm 119:2, 14, 32; James 1:22-25)*

Not that life is always smooth sailing when we obey the Lord. Sometimes obedience costs, and surrender can be painful. But the results are worth every sacrifice.

Obedience to Christ brings eternal rewards.
(Revelation 2:7, 11, 17, 26-20)

This life is but a blink of an eye compared to eternity. *Live today like heaven matters, knowing every decision you make counts beyond what you can see.*

Obedience to Christ releases His power in us to be more than conquerors.

Read Deuteronomy 28:13, and re-write it in your own words.

_____
_____
_____

Can you think of a time when you obeyed the Lord and were glad you did? What happened?

_____
_____
_____

For the most part, obeying the Lord has meant stronger and deeper friendships for me, joy in my work, respect even from unbelievers, and a wonderful marriage.

What incredible blessings! But what about when others oppose you for obeying the Lord?

Losing friends or a job is never fun. But really, the friends I want around me are the ones who encourage me to walk in God's ways, not in sin. And if I lose my job, then it is worth it for the joy of obeying Him. (2 Peter 4:12-19)

There is joy in obedience, no matter how many people oppose you or how difficult the circumstances. (Acts 13:49-52)

Obedience to God may not be rewarded in the way we hope, but He most definitely rewards us with more of Himself when we obey.

The truth is many believers don't walk in enough fear of the Lord or passion for Him to obey Him in everything. (Proverbs 1:7)

God is gentle, abounding in love, and slow to get angry. But He is also *just* and *holy*, and *worthy of obedience*. (Romans 6, Deuteronomy 11, Ephesians 5) **It is dangerous NOT to obey Him.**

Obeying God is not merely adhering to a list of dos and don'ts. (Ephesians 2:8-9) That would be legalism, an enemy stronghold that sucks the life out of you and those around you, because it makes Christianity about doing what is expected of you; rather than enjoying Christ. It makes walking His paths a burden, rather than the joy

Psalm 119 calls it.

Obeying God should be something that flows naturally from the fountain of a passionate love for Him.

The closer you walk with Jesus, the easier it is to obey Him.

John 14:15 says to my heart: *"If you really love Me, you will have no problem obeying Me because it will be all you want to do!"*

I like Matthew 22:37-40, too, because it does away with the list of dos and don'ts. If I love God and love others, then I'll just naturally do all the things He talks about.

"Be doers of the word, and not hearers only, deceiving yourselves." James 1:22

Want to Keep From Falling?

Did you read the Bible today? What did you feel Him asking you to do in the passage you read?
_____
_____
_____

Is there anything God has asked you to do that you haven't done yet? What's keeping you from obedience?
_____
_____
_____

How will you obey Him TODAY?
_____
_____
_____

Get in the habit of looking for His commands each day as you read the Word—like "Fear not," "Praise the Lord," "Be still and know that I am God," etc. Ask God to help you walk out in His Word. The more you obey Him, the closer you get to Him, the louder His voice is, and the easier it is to obey; not to mention the JOY that comes from obedience! There is an inexplicable ecstasy in walking as one with the One who created you. It's like everything that was out of line in your life lines up suddenly, and you have power to walk through, and even soar over, anything.

Dare to Fear the Lord

No Other Eye-Dulls!

The words "fear" and "afraid" appear hundreds of times in the Word, but nearly every verse says one of two things: *"Fear not"* and *"Fear the Lord."*

So why are we afraid of what others think of us, or of messing up, or of being left out, or of what might happen to us, or whatever else it is that keeps our minds busy with worry?

It's an eyes issue. *What are you looking at?*

Are you looking at what you expect to happen or to God who can do anything? Are you looking at your needs or to your Provider? Are you relying on your own abilities or His power? Are you looking to man for approval or to God?

If your eyes are on God and you walk in the confidence that your times are in His hands (Psalm 31:15), **you will be a man of rest, peace and confidence, not a man of fear.** *(2 Timothy 1:7)* Then **He will be the One you "fear,"** *not people or circumstances.*

I guess you could say, almost anything else you focus on can become an *"eye-dull."*

Get it? Idol? Eye-dull? Okay. That's a little corny, but can you see how taking your focus off God and bowing to your fear or self-pity or whatever can block your view of how all-powerful God is and how much He loves you?

Besides that, *idols make Him jealous.* (Exodus 20:3-5) **He's likely to cast down your eye-dull!**

And that's a good thing. You want Him to break off your "heart-wrists" the chains of fear of man (or whatever else attracts your attention), and set you free to love, adore, and "fear" only Him.

There's no way to describe to a prisoner what is on the other side of the bars that confine him. It takes freedom to really, truly *get* it. That's why so many of us continue on in bondage to fears that lead us away from God, rather than just trusting Him.

He might allow some difficult, even painful experiences into our lives to expose the lies that build our prison walls, so He can set us free with His truth.

When that happens, remember you can trust His love and His good purposes. (Hebrews 12:7-13; James 1:2-4)

If you submit to God's discipline, you will find freedom, joy, and the power to walk in victory. (Hebrews 12:7-13)

When I was sick with an incurable disease that promised to leave me blind, insane, in terrible pain, and bed-ridden for the rest of my life, I cried out to God, complaining, "But, Lord! I never thought my life would turn out this way!"

I had planned on taking you and your sister so many wonderful places, and being a great mom and wife and…

"WHOSE life?" God's voice boomed inside my mind.

Trembling, I answered, "Uhh… *Yours,* Lord. I gave my life to *You*." Somehow, in my fear and desperation, I'd forgotten that. But *He* hadn't.

That was an intense fear-of-the-Lord moment I'll never forget! From then on, He began to gently mold me and teach me to *surrender every thought, every hope, every dream — everything — to Him every moment of every day.* (2 Corinthians 10:5)

I trusted Him with the rest of my life, no matter what it looked like, knowing that He would be with me, that He loves me, and that He is *good*.

No matter how bad my circumstances got, I knew **the only truly Safe Place for me was in His arms.**

And then He healed me.

He didn't have to. After all, I had surrendered to whatever He had for me, even if that included blindness, pain and insanity. And He had already filled me with joy and peace, even in the midst of my horrible circumstances. *With Him, I could have made it through anything!*

But what if He allowed that difficulty so I could know Him not just as my Rescuer and Healer, but as my Sovereign? *What if surrendering to His sovereignty was the key to my freedom?*

After all, the trek to the Promised Land was only supposed to take the Israelites a few weeks, not 40 years. If they had trusted in God's faithfulness, rather than complaining, surely they would have made it to the place He was taking them, rather than dying in that desert.

I don't want to die in my desert. Do you?

*Fear of the Lord isn't like any other fear. It is a **safe fear**, a fear that brings peace, rescues, heals, and sets you free.*

Other fears drive us away from what we fear or make us want to defend ourselves against it.

But *fearing the Lord draws you near to Him*, *makes you one with Him, leads you into wise paths, good things, safe places. He can be trusted. He loves you. (Matthew 10:26-31. I John 4:18)*

The Hebrew word used in the Old Testament for *"fear"* holds the idea of awe, reverence, and piety. But its main meaning is fear or terror.

Don't be mistaken, God is not to be trifled with.

Check out Deuteronomy 28. The first 14 verses of blessings for those who worship and obey the Lord are followed by 54 verses of curses that fall on those who don't.

And He is still a God to be feared in the New Testament, as well. See Acts 5:1-11. What happened to those believers who didn't fear the Lord?

_____
_____

Galatians 5:16-21 says that those who are selfish, argumentative, impure, angry, and participate in cliques, among other things, "will not inherit the kingdom of God."

That's a scary list, and a lot of Christians are on it. *None of those things are worth forfeiting your inheritance!*

Are you on that list? If so, take a moment to humble yourself before the Lord and ask Him to set you free from those things. Write Him a prayer from your heart here.

_____
_____
_____
_____
_____

"The fear of man brings a snare, but whoever trusts in the LORD shall be safe."
Proverbs 29:25

Fear of the Lord is a guardrail that keeps me from falling. I wouldn't dare step away from Him to go my own way for fear of losing the peace, blessings, and abundant joy of His felt presence.
(2 Kings 17:7-20)

You see, I can't live even a moment without Him. I crave His voice in my ear, His friendship, His guidance, His touch.

I love to watch Him perform miracles only God can do, the way ***He transforms my ordinary, even awful moments into extraordinary, God-awesome moments.***

I love it when He changes me, sets me free, and uses me for His glory. In fact, I hate my sin because it separates me from Him, and to be one with my Jesus Who loved me and died for me is my only desire.

More than breath or life or anything else, what I long for, what I worship, is God and God alone.

Want to Be Fearless?

Circle a quote from this chapter that impacted you, and write in the margin next to it why.

What do the following verses say about fear of the Lord?

Proverbs 9:10: _____

Proverbs 10:27: _____

Proverbs 14:27: _____

Proverbs 8:13: _____

Proverbs 19:23: _____

What are you worried about or afraid of? Ask God to show you any "eye-dulls" and write what comes to mind.

_____
_____
_____

Have you ever missed an opportunity to share Christ with a lost person because you were afraid of what he or she would think of you? Or wanted to raise your hands in worship but didn't because others might see you? Is there any other way fear has kept you from worshipping God or obeying Him? Ask God, and write what comes to mind.

_____
_____
_____
_____
_____

Now write Him a prayer, laying down all your fears and pledging to fear and worship only the Lord.

_____
_____
_____
_____
_____
_____
_____
_____
_____
_____
_____

"The fear of the Lord is the beginning of wisdom." Psalm 111:10

Get in the habit of leaning on the Lord for everything, surrendering to His will, and seeking His answers to your problems. Ask God to help you re-focus your eyes off of people or circumstances and onto Him, replacing fear with faith.

Dare to Be Humble

11

A Magnet for His Majesty

What was different about Moses' relationship with God? See Numbers 12:6-8.

_____

_____

What was it about Moses that invited God so near? See Numbers 12:3.

_____

_____

You could know the Word, obey God, and seek to serve Him all your life, but without humility, you will miss out on the "more" you were made for.

Humility draws us into God's presence and places us in the right position for intimacy with Him.

Wait! Hold on a second! Moses *wrote* Numbers! So, he said of *HIMSELF* he was "the humblest man in the world." How is *that* humility?

God's definitions don't always match man's.

Humility is not disagreeing with someone who thinks well of you. It's not putting yourself down when you're really quite good at something. Those are earthly definitions.

Humility is agreeing with God.

In other words,

- **feeling like a failure is a form of pride**, because God says you're "more than a conqueror." (Romans 8:37)
- Declining an invitation to preach on the basis of **"I'm not good at that" is also pride**, because Philippians 4:13 says you can do anything through Christ who strengthens you.

Of course, if God tells you to decline from accepting the invitation to preach, that's a totally different ball game! But you won't be doing it because you think whatever about yourself, but rather because you love God and want to obey Him.

God is holy, righteous, omnipotent, omniscient, omnipresent, and your Creator. *He knows what He's talking about.*

Nothing is hidden from Him. When He shows you something, *especially if it's sin*, listen up.

In fact, *the easiest way to break free from a sin stronghold is to see your sin the way God sees it,* **to agree with Him** *about it.*

Let that sin become so repulsive to you, as you sit in the presence of the Holy One you love, that you will never want to do it again.

Humility is surrendering to God.

What does 2 Corinthians 10:3-5 say we should do with our thoughts?

_____

_____

Why is that important? See Isaiah 55:6-9.

_____

_____

_____

So how do you know what God's thoughts are?

By walking close to Him, taking time to listen to His heart in your quiet times, reading the Word, laying down your opinions and ideas at His feet, and asking Him for His.

When we humble ourselves before the Lord, surrendering our thoughts and our ways to His sovereignty, we become one with Him, just as Jesus was one with His Father. (John 14:14-21)

In John 5:19, what does Jesus say about Himself?

_____

_____

Humility is depending on God.

A few years ago, I felt God urging me to teach a Bible study. But in my quiet times, whenever I would ask Him to confirm this urging, His still, small voice answered, "No."

Confused, I asked Him one last time, "Do You want me to teach this study this fall?"

His answer boomed in my head, "No! *I* want to teach it!"

I had asked the wrong question!

So, I rephrased it, "Do You want me to be a warm body in the room while *YOU* teach this Bible study this fall?"

"YES!" came the emphatic reply.

That Bible study turned out to be one of the most amazing experiences ever. The very first night we met together, I had pieced together some worship music about surrender. On the last song, one of the women stood up, trembling and wide-eyed.

"I feel the ground beneath our feet shaking, and I see written in the air, 'I ACCEPT YOUR SURRENDER,'" she said.

And that was just the first night! Every time we got together, God worked miracles in us and all around us.

I'm so glad I surrendered and let *God* be the One in control of that Bible study. I'm so glad I humbled myself before Him and let *HIM* teach.

Humility is always being conscious that you are in the presence of One greater than you.

If God is your everything, the One you live for, then there's no room to spend your thoughts on how incapable you are, because He makes all things possible! (Luke 1:37)

- **Self-pity is a form of pride** because you are focused on what you want that you didn't get.

- **Judgment is a form of pride** because you're focused on someone else's faults, rather than cleaning up your own mess. (Matthew 7:1-5)

- **Looking down on yourself** is a form of pride because your thoughts are all about you, rather than all about God.

Humility is focusing your eyes on God.

Want Grace?

What are the qualities of humility described in Philippians 2:1-16?

_____
_____
_____
_____
_____
_____

What does God do when we're humble? See James 4:6, 10. _____
_____
_____

Go back through this chapter, noting the different definitions of pride bulleted on these last two pages. Have you ever thought those thoughts before? Explain.

_____
_____
_____
_____
_____

Those are some less obvious forms of pride we often tend to overlook because they can *feel* humble. Even judgment, as proud as it looks on this page, can often seem "righteous" when you're in the middle of passing it. "Well, he really *should* ... Don't you agree? I mean, I'm just calling it like it is. I'm sure God's with me on this one!"

What are other forms of pride? Ask God to point some out to you, and write what comes to mind.

- _____
_____
_____

- _____
  _____
  _____

- _____
  _____
  _____

- _____
  _____
  _____

Now write the corresponding forms of humility that rank opposite each of those attitudes.

- _____
  _____
  _____

- _____
  _____
  _____

- _____
  _____
  _____

- _____
  _____
  _____

Do you feel convicted of any pride, or challenged to walk in deeper humility? Look through those bolded, italicized definitions of humility throughout this chapter again, and what you wrote iunder the first paragraph of "Want grace?" Write some ways you feel God leading you to draw nearer to Him through humility.

_____
_____
_____
_____
_____
_____

Recognizing our pride isn't much fun. Everyone likes to think of himself as humble. But stop for a moment and think back on the things you said and thought today. Which of those thoughts began with "I"?

_____
_____
_____
_____

How would your count of "I" thoughts today compare with those beginning with "Jesus ...," "God ..." or "You ..."?

That should spark a new, humble God-sentence right now: "God, *I need You...*"

Notice there's an "I" in that sentence, but it's sandwiched between and *bowed to* the One Who is both the Beginning and the End. (Revelation 22:13) **Fully covered by God is a safe place to be.**

*Humility begins and ends with Jesus. If He is not your Everything, you'll find yourself not only unfulfilled, but **devoured**. (1 Peter 5:5-11)*

Get in the habit of constantly remembering you are in the presence of One greater than you, holier than you, wiser than you, and more powerful than you. *Bow to Him*, for He is your King. What He says is the truth, not what you think or what others say. So get in the habit of agreeing with Him. Let Him show you your sin through His eyes, so pride will no longer bind you to it. Rather, as you see the ways your sin hurts others or damages your relationship with God, you will hate it so much you'll turn away from it. As you walk in humility before God, you will hear His voice and feel His presence stronger than ever before. (James 4:7-10) You will also find yourself more than a conqueror whenever Satan attacks, for he can never win over your heart, as long as you are surrendered to Jesus. (Romans 8:37-39, 16:19-20) The humble man is a triumphant man, because he's surrendered to the Sovereign One.

Part III:
At War

Dare to Know the Truth and Live It

Get Out of Jail!

If you knew you were in prison, wouldn't you want to be free?

Yet, most believers remain captive to lies they believe, and truth they deny. (John 8:42-47)

Spiritually speaking, a "lie" is anything that is contrary to what God says.

Why is feeling you can't do anything right a lie? See Philippians 4:13.

_____
_____
_____

How is feeling anxious a lie? See Philippians 4:4-7.

_____
_____

How is carrying a heavy load of guilt or condemnation a lie? See Romans 8:1 and 1 John 1:9.

_____
_____

How is anger at God for an injustice a lie? See Psalm 9:16.

_____
_____

Lies like these can bind you and control your thoughts and actions. People who feel they're a failure act like one. Anxious people can develop serious physical problems. Anger at God can make you run from Him.

What should we do when we have thoughts that are against the knowledge of God? See 2 Corinthians 10:3-5.

_____
_____
_____

A friend of mine asked me for help with something I had expertise on. But whenever I made suggestions, he spat angry words at me.

A need to prove myself rose to the surface, blaring so loudly in my heart that I excused myself and went to be alone with God.

I asked Him where that feeling came from, and He flooded my mind with memories from my childhood—kids calling me names and banding together to beat me up. *"I must not be important if you treat me this way,"* was the lie that surfaced.

Then I asked Him for His truth, and in those sweet moments alone with God, He reminded me that I am royalty, a daughter of the King of Kings. I have no need to prove my worth, for I am already precious, beloved—not because of what I know or how good I am at this or that, but because of Who my Father is.

As far as I know, the need to prove myself has never returned. God set me free!

Now, don't you think I had read the Bible before He showed me this? Don't you think I already knew I was His daughter?

*You can know the truth in your head, but **until that truth changes you, you are still a captive. It has to go deep into the inmost place. (Psalm 51:6)** And **that only happens through a close encounter with the One whose name is Truth. (John 14:6)***

"If you abide in My Word, you are My disciples indeed. And **you shall know the truth, and the truth shall make you free.**" John 8:31-32

Every encounter with Jesus is different. But I can give you some suggestions to open the door for Him to bring you healing and freedom through His truth:

1. *Use the Galatians 5:22-23 gauge.*
   - Notice when you're angry, afraid, depressed, or discontent. Such feelings are contrary to the peace, love, joy, etc., that are yours in Christ in those verses. Then, politely *excuse yourself* from the person or situation and *find a place where you can be alone with God.*
   - *Ask Him where the negative feeling comes from.* Don't just say, "I'm mad because that guy said thus-and-so!" *Don't look at what someone else did wrong; look at what's going on in your own heart.*
   - Let God show you anything He wants, and just go with Him there. *Look for the lies.* Then *ask Him for His truth*.
   - Keep your heart open during the days and weeks ahead. Don't give up if He doesn't show you something right away. *You're on a journey. It's not only about getting there; the road is just as important.*

2. *Do a Word Search.*
   - *Look up in a concordance* (there are free ones online) *all the verses that have to do with your issue.* For example, if you're struggling with fear, look up all the verses with the words "fear" or "afraid," and the opposite as well, "faith" or "trust."
   - Keep a journal of all the things God's showing you through His Word about your issue, and purpose to walk out in the truth and in obedience to Him.

Knowing what the Word says and walking in the truth will not only mean freedom from the pain that lies cause, but also greater intimacy with Christ, which is what you were created for.

Get in the habit of checking your thoughts. Listen to yourself sometime: What were you thinking when you did that? Were you being selfish ("I need that!")? Were you pushing an agenda that God hasn't asked you to push ("They should do it my way!")? Were you judging ("He really *should...*")?

Know what the Word says and live it.

Also, *be faithful to speak truth in a spirit of love and from the Word to others so that the body of Christ can be built up and mature in Him.* (Ephesians 4:15) It's possible many will oppose you. Even Christians don't always like to hear truth, especially when their lies have become "comfortable" to them. But Jesus met with opposition for speaking truth, so you're in good company.

Through everything in life, don't lean on your own understanding, but seek the Lord. Find out what He says about it; then live that truth.
Proverbs 3:5-6.

Jesus said, "I am the way, the truth, and the life." John 14:6a

Want Things to Change?

Use the Galatians 5:22-23 gauge today to clean out your heart.

1. Think about the last time you felt angry, discouraged, afraid or whatever emotion comes to mind that is contrary to the love, joy, peace, patience, kindness, goodness, faithfulness, gentleness, self-control that are yours in Christ.

2. Ask God where that feeling came from. Remember not to look at what the other person said or did, but only look at your own heart. *Pointing fingers at someone else is the best way to miss what God is showing you.* Ask God why you felt that way in that situation. He may bring a memory to mind of something that happened when you were a child. Or He may tell you something you believe that is contrary to His Word.

3. Don't dismiss it. Instead, *allow yourself to remember, to feel what you felt when that happened, or when you first believed that.*

4. Let Jesus show you what the lies are that you believe and how they entered your heart (like

"I'm all alone," "No one will ever love me as much as I love them," "I'm such a failure," "I'm stupid," "I'll never measure up," "No one likes me," etc.)

5. Then ask Him to show you His truth. Ask Him what He thinks about what happened to you at that time or about the lies you believed. He might show you what He was doing or saying in the midst of that trial. Or He might remind you of a verse that is the truth that opposes your lie.

6. Run what you feel Him saying to you through the Three-Fold sieve from chapter 8:

- Does it line up with the Word?
- Does it line up with His character?
- Does it draw you closer to Him?

Now, as you seek to walk out in the truth of what He just showed you today, spend time in your quiet times each day looking up in a concordance all the verses that have to do with that, and recording in your journal what He's showing you. For example, if your lie was, "Everyone who loves me leaves me," you might look up "leave" or "forsake," and also verses on "trust" and "faithful."

Don't let a lie control you rather than the Holy Spirit. (John 8:42-47, Galatians 5:1, 22-25) Get in the habit of taking all your negative feelings to the Lord, looking for the lies contrary to the Word that caused them, and letting God topple those lies with His truth that sets you free. Don't waste this trial. Let God change you. Then you will SOAR over it with joy, because you're riding on the wings of the One who knows where He's taking you. (Exodus 19:4)

Dare to Defy Enemy Schemes

13

Double Agent? No!

What if you and your friend were secret service agents and the enemy came to you and said, "Hey, why don't you betray the King and double cross your partner?" You'd say, *"No way!"*

But our enemy isn't so blatant. He *sneaks* in. He might disguise himself and defend you in a jam. Then he might say subtle things here and there to indicate your partner is a double agent.

You begin to notice things that confirm that idea. At last, with your conscience clear that you're protecting your country, you sabotage one of your partner's missions, turning him in as a traitor.

Now who's the double agent, working both for the King and for your enemy? Did you set out to do that? No, of course not.

> "Be sober, be vigilant; because your adversary the devil walks about like a roaring lion, seeking whom he may devour. Resist him, steadfast in the faith..." 1 Peter 5:8-9a

This actually happens often in the spiritual realm: You have a real enemy—Satan—who is out to destroy those who follow Jesus. And he most often uses God's own people to do it. He is so sneaky about it; in fact, *we think we're obeying God.*

How many churches have split, each side thinking they're right? How many Christian relationships have broken apart?

If you're on the alert, you might be able to discern when the enemy's attacking and even what he's doing: *he's discouraging you, dividing a friendship, wanting you to wallow in self-pity, trying to make you lose your temper and hurt someone, keeping you from doing what God wants...*

But no matter what the enemy is doing, **God is doing much, much more.**

In fact, God is so Sovereign that even the enemy is subject to Him! That means Satan can't attack unless God allows it. And if God allows it, then it is because He is doing something good.

One time, something happened between your father and me. I can't remember what it was, but I remember feeling God urging me to apologize. Your dad's reaction was so defensive that I asked him, "What do you think I just said?"

The sentence he quoted back to me *rhymed* with my sentence *word for word*, but it was an *accusation*, not an apology! **The enemy had twisted my words in the air!**

Rather than fighting against each other, we prayed and *fought against misunderstanding and dissension*. We grew closer to each other and closer to the Lord, and have taught other couples the things we've learned through that strange trial. **What the enemy meant for evil, God used for good.**

Don't miss out on the hidden treasures and eternal rewards God has prepared for you in every trial. **Find out what God's doing and join Him there.**

If you're not sure what He's doing, at least **purpose to do the opposite of what the enemy is doing.**

For instance, if you're tempted to complain, *thank God instead.* If you feel depressed, *worship God.* If you're angry at someone, *pray for him and bless him.* (Romans 12:14, 17-21; Philippians 2:14-16)

What does Proverbs 3:5-7 say to your heart?

_____
_____

Surrendering to God *is your key to winning every battle.*

Don't just say, "Oh, God must be teaching me

patience," and then resume your old ways when the trial is all done.

If the battle doesn't change you, you will find yourself on the same battlefront over and over again until you "get it."

God loves you enough to do whatever it takes to knock down the idols and strongholds that keep you from living life to its fullest in Him.

It takes the friction of scrubbing against the grain of the fabric of who you used to be to release those stubborn stains and make you the person God made you to be.

And friction can be very uncomfortable. It may feel easier just to lose your temper and say, "That's just how I am." But once you can clearly see how the enemy uses you when you're angry to hurt those around you, you might opt out of the double-agent deal and let God set you free.

Once God sets you free, the battle in that area of your life usually ends, because the enemy loses a lot of ground when he tries to "press your buttons" and all that comes out of you is Jesus.

Oh, he'll find other ways to wage war against you, and you'll live to fight another day.

But if you get in the habit of opposing the enemy by surrendering to what God is doing in every battle, Satan will lose, and you'll pile up treasure!

Also, don't underestimate what God might be doing in the hearts of others through your trial. What if someone comes to the Lord? What if God uses you to draw other believers closer to Him?

Doing what God is doing brings eternal results.

Want to Fight on the Right Side?

What difficult circumstances are you facing now?

_____

_____

_____

What does it seem the enemy could be doing in these circumstances?

_____

_____

_____

How can you do the opposite?

_____

_____

_____

Ask God, "What are You doing? How can I join you there?" Write whatever comes to mind.

_____

_____

_____

_____

Again, don't worry if you can't hear His answer straight away. The important thing is to ask Him, and to leave your heart open before Him. Be sure and check for any sin or lies that might be blocking you from hearing His voice. *If you walk close to Him, trusting Him to answer you and guide you, then you won't miss what He's doing.*

He is usually doing many things, so don't stop at just one answer. Most specifically, ask Him what He is doing *in your heart*, and how He is drawing you closer to Himself.

Is there any attitude, sin, or thought process in you that's been exposed through this trial that the Lord might want to set you free from? Ask Him where that attitude or sin comes from, let Him show you the lies, and then His truth.

Don't waste this trial. Surrender to the Lord and His purposes. Let Him change you and set you free from the things within you that made the trial so difficult. Then next time a similar trial comes, you will soar over it on wings of freedom.

Get in the habit of doing the opposite of what the enemy is doing in every circumstance. Look for what God is doing, and go there with Him.

Dare to Fight for the Things that Matter

To Fight or Not to Fight

One day, I was helping at church, and the woman in charge took a task away from her teenage daughter and handed it over to me.

Thinking the young girl might feel hurt, I tried to encourage her by telling her how well she was doing at so many things I would make a mess of. It was lame, I'll admit, but it was all I could think of at the moment.

Later, the girl disappeared, and her father marched up to me screaming, "You should have given her that task! How dare you! You must apologize to her for the mean things you said!"

Mean things? You can imagine what I was thinking. It went something like, "Well, how dare you! Your wife told her to give the job to me, and I was just following her orders. She's the one you should be yelling at! You've got a problem with anger, mister! And besides, I was being *nice* to your daughter!"

But as fast as I could, I dumped all those thoughts into Jesus' lap, and then said to the man, "What time can I come by this afternoon to apologize?"

I knew I needed to fight for the things that matter, and my pride isn't one of those things! A wounded teenager is.

I'll admit, I was scared—not of the sweet daughter, but of her Doberman dad. It's my experience that angry people just get angrier when you apologize; I feared facing a monster!

So I got on my face before the Lord. Through the next couple of hours before the ominous meeting, I laid down all my thoughts and opinions at Jesus' feet and asked for His.

He began to show me all the wonderful things He loves about this teenager I barely knew—how she loved Him so much she was willing to do the things no one else would for Him, how precious she was to Him, beloved.

By the time I got to her home, I had to kneel on the floor at her feet. I felt so honored to be in the presence of one He loved so much. I said, "Please forgive me," and then told her all the beautiful things God had said about her.

He used the opportunity to speak into her life and pour out His love over her in a way that would carve how she saw herself as a daughter of Christ for years to come.

But my task wasn't over. I felt the Lord say, "Now I want to speak to the father."

My heart raged, "Sure! I'll give him a piece of Your mind for You! That guy's got serious anger issues!"

But when I opened my mouth to speak, the Holy Spirit that flowed out surprised me. I found myself saying, "God wants you to know He saw what happened to you when you were a child. Now you have become a defender of the little ones, and He stands beside you."

That was a turn of events I never saw coming!

You have an enemy, but it's not your brother. So **fight FOR your brother, not against him.**
(Ephesians 6:12)

The battle is not to prove you're right, or get your brother to agree with you, or make him do what you want, but *to expose Satan's schemes and lies so God can set you both free from the things you're captive to.* (2 Corinthians 10:3-5)

In such spiritual battles, your weapons are not of this world. Wear your armor of truth, peace, and righteousness (Ephesians 6:14) and wield your sword, which is the Word of God (Ephesians 6:17). Remember that *it is in prayer that the battle is won* (Ephesians 6:18).

Notice how I prayed and God changed my heart *before* I engaged outwardly in the battle. That way, I could come in line with what God was doing, rather than what the enemy was doing.

What do you think the enemy might have been doing in that situation?

_____
_____
_____

What did God do? (Don't write just one thing. Remember, *God is always doing many things. But no matter what He's doing, He's always drawing us closer to Himself.* So, write the things you saw Him doing in others, but also what He did in me.)

_____
_____
_____
_____
_____
_____
_____

When Jesus turned over the tables at the temple (Mark 11:15-17), He didn't do it on a whim or in uncontrolled rage. *He looked around the day before* (Mark 11:11) *and waited until the next day to act on what he saw.*

Likewise, it is good for you not to lash out immediately at someone you're angry with. Rather, take time to get with the Lord and let your thoughts come in line with His (Isaiah 55:6-9). Check your own heart out and make sure the sin isn't actually yours (Matthew 7:1-5).

Then when you finally approach others about sin, as in Matthew 18:15, you will do it with a humble heart, speaking the truth in love (Ephesians 4:15), and with the purpose of *fighting for their freedom.*

Make sure you know the facts before you accuse. Only God knows what your brother is thinking and only He is Judge over his motives.

(James 4:11-12) So, it's a good idea to talk with your friend first to *find out why he did something, and ask the Lord how He sees the situation before you accuse.*

You want to be on the side of the One whose name is Love (1 John 4:16) and Truth (John 14:6), not the one whose name is Accuser (Revelation 12:10) and Father of Lies (John 8:44).

Don't worry if you mess up. Everyone misunderstands sometimes or loses his temper and says things he shouldn't. But when that happens, *be quick to ask forgiveness of the person you hurt.*

And get with the Lord. Let Him clean out your heart. You may have a stronghold you need to be set free from, and *this very event might have happened for your freedom!*

Choose your battles well.

How to squeeze the toothpaste or whether the top is put back on aren't issues worth getting angry about. Likewise, opinions or politics or sports teams or anything else—if they aren't eternal issues founded in the Word, they aren't worth losing friendships over. (James 4:1-3)

Want to Win that Fight?

What do we fight for? See Psalm 45:3-7; 1 Timothy 1:18-19; 6:11-12.

_____
_____
_____

What is the prize? See 2 Timothy 4:7-8.

_____
_____

What "battles" are you facing this week?

_____
_____
_____

Write what Exodus 14:14 and says to your heart.

_____
_____
_____

Think about the last time you experienced a relationship conflict. How did you respond?
_____
_____
_____

Are you in a conflict right now? What is it?
_____
_____
_____

If you're in a conflict now, or know of an unresolved conflict in the past, pause a moment to work through the following steps in your heart with the Lord:

1. **Be quick to listen, slow to speak, and slow to get angry.** (James 1:19)

2. Don't just react. Take time to get in line with God and **make sure your thoughts are His thoughts, and your ways His.** (Mark 11:11-17; Proverbs 3:5-7; Isaiah 55:6-9)

3. **Check out your own heart.** Is there any sin in there? Judgment? Pride? Accusation? Laziness? Did you do something that might have caused the conflict? (Matthew 7:1-5; Isaiah 38:17)

4. If so, **ask forgiveness**, with a heart of love and humility. (1 John 1:8-10)

5. **NO MIND-READING.** Don't just jump to conclusions and accuse someone of something before you find out what the truth is. You can't read someone's mind, so don't think you know what they're thinking or why they said what they did. *Only God and the person know that.* Instead, *pray and ask God what's going on. Ask that person: "When you said…, did you mean…?"* Jesus' name is Truth and Love. But when you falsely accuse someone, you are working for the enemy, whose name is Accuser and Father of Lies. (John 8:42-47; Revelation 12:10-11; Isaiah 59:12-13; Jude 9-10)

6. **Put on your spiritual armor.** (See Ephesians 6:10-20, and the next chapter below) And don't forget your sword. What does the Word say about your situation? Let the Spirit guide you through this conflict.

7. **Choose to do the opposite of what the enemy is doing.** Is he making you angry at those people? Then *forgive them and pray for them.* Is he causing division? Then *step towards them in love.* Is he discouraging you? Then *worship.* Is he manipulating you to do something you don't want to do? Then *do what God wants you to do instead.*

8. **Pray and ask God what He's doing, so you can come in line with His purposes in this conflict.** Is He asking you to be still before Him, and let Him fight this one for you? (Exodus 14:14) Is He asking you to step out and love those who are fighting against you? (Romans 12) ***Whatever He's doing, He is most certainly drawing you closer to Himself.*** So draw close to Him, as well. *Lean into Him through this trial, telling Him how you feel, listening for His voice, letting Him walk before you, beside you, behind you, and in you.* (Exodus 33:14; Exodus 23:20-22; Exodus 9:16; Isaiah 42:13; Isaiah 58:8-9)

9. **Forgive.** (Mark 11:25) ***Remember, you have a real enemy, but it's not your brother. Fight FOR your brother against the enemy.*** Intercede for him, love him, show him mercy. (Romans 12)

Obey the Lord, and you will come out on top in every battle. (Deuteronomy 28:13-14)

Get in the habit of **checking your own heart out first** *before you point your finger at someone else. You can't change that person anyway, but you can change. Let Jesus show you why you feel or react that way, so you can find the sin or wrong thought processes that take you there. Then repent. Let Him replace any lies with His truth, and change you. You just might see that when you change, miraculously the people around you change as well.*

Dare to Cover Over and Armor Up

15

Lookin' Good!

Imagine attending a fashion show for the latest styles for godly men. According to Colossians 3:5-14, what clothes are oout?

_____
_____
_____
_____

What are the "in" clothes you should wear?

_____
_____
_____
_____

In the spiritual realm, the clothing you wear defines who you are.

Why? What does Romans 13:14 say we should clothe ourselves with? _____

How does that make us different from the world?
_____
_____

A believer clothed in humility (1 Peter 5:5) and wearing all his spiritual armor (Ephesians 6:10-18) is less likely to be devoured by our enemy (1 Peter 5:8) than a rebellious man (Isaiah 1:5-6) who left all his clothing and armor at home.

"**Be strong in the Lord and in the power of His might**. Put on the **whole armor of God**, that you may be able to **stand** against the wiles of the devil. For we do not wrestle against flesh and blood, but against principalities, against powers, **against the rulers of the darkness** of this age, against spiritual hosts of wickedness in the heavenly places. Therefore take up the **whole armor of God**, that you may be able to **withstand** in the evil day, and having done all, to **stand**. **Stand** therefore, having girded your waist with **truth**, having put on the breastplate of **righteousness**, and having shod your feet with the preparation of the **gospel of peace**; above all, taking the shield of **faith** with which you will be able to quench all the fiery darts of the wicked one. And take the helmet of **salvation**, and the sword of the **Spirit**, which is the **Word of God**; **praying** always with all **prayer** and supplication in the Spirit, being **watchful** to this end with all **perseverance**." Ephesians 6:10-18

How are we made strong in the battle? What is our power source? (See verse 10) _____

Why must we wear the "whole armor"? What one word is repeated over and over to us as a command in those verses? __ __ __ __ __

PUTTING ON THE WHOLE ARMOR OF GOD:

1. **The Belt of Truth.** In ancient Roman days, the belt bound up a soldier's robes so the folds wouldn't get in the way and hinder his movement. As we saw in Chapter 1, *lies (John 8:43-47) and sin (Hebrews 12:1-3) can hinder us from **walking in the truth of who we are in Christ**, entangling us and tripping us up, rather than letting us **freely move in the Spirit and in Truth**.* (John 8:31-32)

   Ask God what's tripping you up these days, and what His truth is that will bind that lie and keep us from sinning. Write what He shows you here. _____
   _____
   _____

2. **The Breastplate of Righteousness.** Proverbs 4:23 advises us to guard our heart "above all." Why? What "treasure" do we have in our hearts that makes us undefeatable? (See Matthew 6:21, 2 Corinthians 4:6-10, Romans 8:35-39) _____

_____.
Now you know why the enemy goes for our chest. Don't give in to enemy schemes to distance you from God. Whenever the enemy attacks your treasure — your relationship with Christ — let the breastplate of righteousness cover you. Not your own righteous acts, but the right-standing you have with God because of *what Christ has done for you*. Remember Whose you are and why. In what ways has the enemy tried to hit your relationship with Christ? (Busyness? Anger with God? Dry quiet times? Distracting thoughts? Doubt?)
_____
_____

How will you choose to respond? _____
_____
_____

3. **The Shoes of the Preparation of the Gospel of Peace.** In combat, a soldier must be prepared at any moment for attack. That means he often *sleeps with his boots on*. Then when his commander calls, he can jump straight up and fight, no fumbling around for his boots in the dark. In the same way, we prepare ourselves for battle by not just having a quiet time every day, but *walking in step with the Spirit* all throughout the day, whether we feel like we're in a battle or not. (Galatians 5:25) You see, peace isn't something we can conjure up ourselves. It comes from **a lifestyle of surrender to God.** *Combat boots of peace walk us into the war zones of dissensions and arguments, difficulties and trials with a prayerful and thankful heart that overcomes the battle through the power of His love* (Philippians 4:4-7). What does Isaiah 52:7 say about our feet when we bring the good news of peace? _____
_____

4. **The Shield of Faith.** In Roman times, shields were often large enough to cover a soldier's whole body. In the same way, faith in God covers us fully, because He alone is our Shield that puts out the "fire" of the enemy's attacks. (Ephesians 6:16) Faith is also a weapon against the enemy, a ***ramming wall that knocks him down.*** Trusting in God's sovereignty, goodness, faithfulness and love has won many a battle for me. But anytime I try to protect myself (by defending my actions to others or avoiding a situation or any other way I let my fear rule my actions rather than the Holy Spirit), I end up wounded, and sometimes even taken captive (like to fear, pride, defensiveness, unforgiveness, anger, etc.). But with God, I can move a mountain! Read Matthew 17:20, and write the verse into a prayer asking God to increase your faith.
_____
_____
_____
_____

5. **The Helmet of Salvation.** What does a helmet cover? _____. In 1 Corinthians 4:4, what does the enemy do to unbelievers who don't have this helmet? _____
_____

As believers, how are our minds different? (See 1 Corinthians 2:16) _____
_____. So, why do we so often forget to live that truth, and entertain thoughts from the enemy instead? Because in this fight against our enemy, **the battlefield is our minds.** *It's not our situation or what someone else around us does that wounds us or disturbs our peace so much as our reaction — the thoughts that lead us to dark places of doubt, rejection, despair, depression, anger, bitterness, lust, worry, etc.* The helmet of salvation protects our mind from enemy attacks on our thought life. How? What does Romans 12:2 command us to do and why? _____
_____
_____

6. **The Sword of the Spirit, the Word of God.** Read Luke 4:1-12, 2 Timothy 3:16-17 and Hebrews 4:12, and explain why it's important for us to memorize the Word and know it well.
_____

Don't Want to Get Caught Naked?

Write about a time when God brought a Scripture to mind just at the right moment to help you overcome a "battle." _____
_____
_____
_____
_____

Ask God what verse He wants you to memorize next to prepare you for something yet to come. Write the reference here: _____

Look back over the list of clothing (paragraph 2) and armor (numbers 1-6). What are you wearing well? What do you need more of? Spend time in prayer, asking Jesus to clothe you and armor you *completely* with Himself.

_____
_____
_____

In the spiritual realm, our armor is not just a metaphor. It is REAL. The enemy can see where we're vulnerable, and that is where he strikes.

Look up the following verses and write the reference in the margin next to the piece of armor each verse corresponds to: John 14:6; Psalm 27:1; John 1:1, 14; 1 Corinthians 1:30; Psalm 3:3; Ephesians 2:14. Did you notice? Each of the pieces of our armor are a name for _____ .

"Put on the armor of light... Clothe yourselves with the Lord Jesus Christ... Because **when we are clothed, we will not be found naked.**"
Romans 13:12-14; 2 Corinthians 5:3

The enemy can see when you've dropped your armor, and he will attack you wherever you are most exposed. So get in the habit of having a quiet time every day so you will know the Word well and be clothed with Christ Himself. (Romans 13:14) Then you will be more than a conqueror no matter what battles you face. (Romans 8:35-39)

Dare to Walk by Faith

Moving those Mountains

"He who believes in Me, the works that I do he will do also; and greater works than these he will do.... Whatever you ask in My name, that I will do." John 14:12-13

I remember one Fourth of July, when you were about seven years old. You really wanted to see fireworks. But we were traveling and wouldn't be in the right place at the right time. So you asked God to see fireworks. Within minutes, the sky lit up, flashes of lightning all around our car in the most spectacular display of His glory!

But He didn't stop there. As we started over a river, traffic jammed, and we had to stop the car in the middle of the bridge because of the fireworks. *God gave us the best view in the city!*

I know now why Jesus said we must be like little children. (Mark 10:13-16) Children have no problem believing that God can do anything, that their heavenly Daddy is the biggest, strongest, most loving and powerful of all. **My son, don't ever lose your childlike faith in God.**

Satan loves to sow seeds of doubt. In Jesus' case, he even used Scripture to do it (misapplied, of course). Each of the temptations the enemy fired at Jesus in Matthew 4:1-11 begins with *"If...?"* But Jesus won with truth: *"It is written..."*

Don't give in to doubt. (James 1:2-8) *God is and always has been sovereign, wise, good, slow to anger, forgiving, just, merciful, all-powerful, and everything else Scripture says He is. And you are beloved, accepted by Him.*

If God is asking you to do something, He is faithful to do it. You might doubt your own ability, but never, ever doubt God's power or love. (1 Corinthians 2:4-5. Colossians 1:28-29. Philippians 4:13. 2 Corinthians 12:9-10)

Your faith should be in God, not in circumstances, others, or yourself, and not even in what you want God to do.

One woman I mentored a few years ago struggled with trusting her husband. We did a Word Search to find all the verses on "trust." Guess what we found? Hundreds say, *"Trust in the Lord..."* And only a handful say, *"Don't trust in man," "Don't trust in armies," "Don't trust in riches,"* etc.

In other words, trusting anything other than God isn't even supposed to be a thought. Not that I shouldn't trust my husband or friend. Just, *I trust God. Period.*

Rest in the assurance that God is in control, that He is good, that He will bring the best out of every circumstance. *(Romans 8:28)*

How does faith in God make the impossible possible? See Matthew 21:21-22.

_____
_____

God is so God. Believe that He can and will perform a miracle, *but don't be surprised if the miracle isn't what you expect it to be.* You may have faith for God to heal someone physically, but He may heal him spiritually; or the miracle might even be something He does in your own heart as you pray.

Jesus asked God to take the cup of suffering from Him, but His faith was in God, not in God releasing Him from death on the cross. **He qualified His request with surrender to God's will.** (Mark 14:38)

If God calls you to be a missionary in a war-torn country, will He protect you and your family? Most certainly! The protection may be physical or it may be spiritual. You may indeed face torture or death for His name's sake. But remember this:

The safest place to be is in God's hands.

Don't fear what people may do to you. (Luke 12:4-7) This life is short anyway, and full of difficulties no matter what country you live in. *Trust in God, follow Him wherever He leads, love Him with all your heart, and live as if heaven is your home.*

A man of faith is a man at rest because his eyes are on the Lord. (Isaiah 30:15; Joshua 1:9; 2 Chronicles 20:12) *He knows in Whom he trusts.*

Did you notice **Jesus *slept* in the raging storm first, and *then* He calmed it?** (Matthew 8:23-27)

Trust in the Lord who holds all things in His hands, and your heart will be at rest no matter what rages about you.

Up until a few years ago, most sick people actually got worse when I prayed for them. My lack of the gift of healing was so pronounced, in fact, that I began to fear my prayers were the culprit.

Of course, the lie in there is obvious. *Whether or not a person is healed does not depend on my prayer skills or my gifting or even my faith (see that word "my"?), but on the ONE WHO HEALS.*

Anyway, as God began clearing out sin and lies in my heart, I noticed that His voice got louder, and the leading of His Spirit stronger. In fact, all the gifts became available to me. But not as mine; as *His* gifts He gave *whenever He wanted to move.*

So, one night, as a group of us prayer walked a Buddhist temple in our neighborhood, one of the men cried out in pain and couldn't move. He had injured his knee a couple of weeks earlier, and intercessors had prayed for him to no avail. Now his injury had inflamed and the pain was unbearable.

Surrounded by Buddhist monks chanting to demons, and throngs of people bowing to idols, I laid my hand on his knee and spoke out the words I felt God saying. *And God healed him!*

But He did more than that. He declared in the midst of His enemies that HE ALONE IS GOD. And He showed me *He can move the mountains in my heart!*

The key to asking for something in Jesus' name is to walk so closely with Him that you know His heart. *(John 14:10-21) **Then when He wants to perform a miracle, you won't miss the show!***

Want to Move a Mountain?

Ask God if there's anything blocking your faith. Be still before Him, and let Him show you anything He wants to show you. As you look for what might be strangling your faith, doubt and fear are a good place to start, as both of these are enemy opposites of faith. Ask God if there's any way you doubt Him, or anything you're afraid of. Look for the lies, and then ask Him for His truth. Write what comes to mind.

_____
_____
_____
_____
_____
_____

Make sure you run it through the three-fold sieve (Does what you feel Him saying line up with the Word? Does it line up with God's character, especially His love? Does it draw you closer to Him?) Now ask Him to help you believe. (Mark 9:14-32)

What difficult decisions or circumstances are you or someone you know facing?

_____
_____
_____

Ask God what He wants to do, pray as He leads, and trust Him for the outcome. Believe Him to do something miraculous, even if it's not the miracle you're looking for.

Get in the habit of walking so close to Jesus that you know what His heart is, so when you pray it is through His Spirit. Ask Him for the big things, as well as the small, and expect an answer that just might blow you away. (John 15:7)

Dare to Be Filled with the Spirit

What Are You Full of?

We were prayer walking in a closed country, when my friend felt compelled by the Spirit to go down a certain street, where he happened upon a funeral. He walked through the open door, laid his hands on the dead man, prayed, and the man sat up, ALIVE!

A man filled with the Spirit is a powerful man, not in his own strength, but in God's.

The Spirit gives the power to heal, to raise from the dead, to topple strongholds, to lead people to faith, to speak to nations and rulers, to break down walls of prejudice, to change a situation from bad to good, and even to change the world.

Yes, one man walking in the Spirit can leave quite an everlasting imprint.

Have you ever met Christians who overflow with the Spirit? When they speak, you can feel Him moving. When they worship, you can feel His touch. As they walk through life, the lives of others are changed around them.

How did they get that way?

If you live surrendered to God, then His Spirit will flow through you. And if you expect Him to show up, He just might leave you awestruck.

So many people block out the movement of the Holy Spirit because they are afraid of being out of control, or imagining things, or even giving control to Satan. Have you ever felt that way? Explain.

_____
_____
_____
_____

God is a gentleman, and if you don't want Him to do something miraculous, speak to you, or work through you, He just might not. (Matthew 9:23-25)

The places where God most often shows up in power are the places where believers are expecting Him to do just that.

Some Christians believe that if you speak in tongues, you're filled with the Spirit; and if you can't, then you aren't. But I've met Christians who boast speaking in tongues, yet are bitter toward others; and other believers without that gift who are loving and humble, drawing people to God.

The proof of being filled with the Spirit is not in the gift, but in the fruit. (Galatians 5:22-23)

Think about it. When you apply pressure to a spray can, what comes out? Whatever's in the can!

So if anger or pride is what you're full of, that is what will come out under pressure. But if Jesus is what you're full of, His Spirit will flow out of you.

If you want to be Spirit-filled, a good place to start is to invite Him.

Before you read from the Word, ask Him to speak to your heart; then look for what He's saying.

When you speak to a crowd, ask God to guide you, and trust Him that He's doing so. Don't worry about messing up. He is Lord even over your mistakes.

Again, remember that **anything the Spirit leads you to do must line up with the Word and God's character, and draw people to Him** (our Threefold Sieve from chapter 8).

Galatians 5:25 urges us to "keep in step" with the Spirit by being about what God is about, doing the things He is doing, rather than doing the things the world does. (See all of Galatians 5.)

If you are all about God, loving Him with all your

heart, spending time in His Word and at His feet, and walking out in what He asks of you, you will live a Spirit-empowered life.

Check out Colossians 1:28-29 and 1 Corinthians 2:4-5. Why do you think it's important for the Spirit to lead us?

_____

_____

I like to begin each day with surrender to God, even before I get out of bed. Then I have the joy of spending the day watching Him do amazing things and joining Him in them.

One morning, as I awoke in the dark country where we work, I asked the Lord as usual, "What do You want to do today?"

His answer came powerfully and specifically. At 8:30 a.m., I was to call a local believer, Isaiah, who lived in another town, pick him up, and take him to a certain village.

Now, reason rose up in me and I argued, "But Isaiah doesn't even know me. Besides, I'm a woman, and that's just weird. And furthermore, no one in that village will be there. They're all at a festival." But I surrendered to God anyway, trusting He would close the door if it wasn't His plan.

At 8:30, I called Isaiah, half hoping he wouldn't answer. But he did, and a couple of hours later, we were chatting face to face. I told him about the village where two people in one family had come to Christ.

He quieted and looked intently into my face. "You want me to go there with you, don't you?" Then he stood up, grabbed his backpack, and reached for his hidden stash of tracts, asking, "What do we take with us?"

Reason spoke out again: "Well, they can't read or write, so maybe we should just take some fruit."

Besides, carrying religious materials was dangerous in that area; we could be arrested, or worse.

Then, the Holy Spirit convicted me, and I blurted out. "No! *Pray!* And then take whatever *God* tells you to take." I watched as he grabbed some booklets and stuffed them in his backpack.

When we arrived at the village, a daughter I had never met because she attended school in another village was there with several of her classmates, preparing to go to the festival. They eagerly listened as we storied from creation all the way through Christ.

All eight of the girls came to the Lord that day! And every one of them could read. When Isaiah opened his backpack, *he had exactly eight booklets on growing as new believers, no more, no less.*

At each turn throughout the day, I had the choice to be led by the Spirit or by my flesh and reason. The consequences of my choices were eternal.

Want God to Take the Lead?

What is God's command in Ephesians 5:18b?

_____

Spend some time in worship today (play the guitar, sing, listen to your favorite worship music, read some psalms, or whatever He's leading you to do). Focus your heart on the Lord.

Then lay all your responsibilities at His feet. Ask God to fill you with His Spirit and anoint you to carry out each thing in the power of His leading. Write your prayer here.

_____

_____

_____

_____

_____

Get in the habit of surrendering your heart to God every moment. Ask Him for His opinions and ideas, so He can replace yours with His. Ask Him what He wants you to do, rather than just doing whatever you feel like doing whenever. Let Him truly be your Lord, Master, and King. Then He will fill you with His Spirit, and when the enemy "presses your buttons," all that comes out of you is Jesus!.

Dare to Shrink Not from Death

Dying to Live

Paul's claim of finding joy in sharing in the sufferings of Christ used to baffle me. But not any longer. The closer I walk with Jesus, the more I'm finding the ecstasy of hearing His voice and standing in His footprints, speaking His words no matter what it costs.

I'm not kidding, He actually *fills me with joy when people attack me*—not because they attack me, but because *He is with me and I am free*. No one, nothing, can smack chains on me when my eyes are fixed on Him!

His truth is such a spacious place to stand that it gives us immunity from enemy attacks. Not that the enemy won't attack, because he most certainly will. But he just can't win. Even the pain of losing a friend is nothing compared to the joy of following Christ and running in His paths.

2 Timothy 3:12 says that everyone who wants to live a godly life will be persecuted. It's not a "maybe" or a "hopefully not," but a promise you can count on.

John 15:20 reminds us that we are no greater than our Master, Jesus. If He endured persecution for His love for God and obedience to Him, then we His servants can expect it also.

Our hope, our joy, in Christ is that every trial, every persecution, every difficulty we face in this life will gain us eternal rewards if we keep our eyes fixed on Him and go through the trial His way.
(2 Corinthians 4:17-18; James 1:2-4)

Before we moved overseas, as your father and I received reports of persecution of believers in the area of the world where God was calling us, I remember crying out to Him, "How do they do it? I don't know that I'm strong enough to go through torture and solitary confinement for You."

He answered, "You know you would much rather be in a jail cell *with Me* than anywhere else without Me."

And He's right. I know that **the safest place to be is in His arms.** He is my Everything. Without Him, life holds nothing for me.

"For to me, to live is Christ, and to die is gain."
Philippians 1:21

Persecution may mean physical death, as it does in many places throughout the world. Or it may mean death to your reputation or a relationship or your job or your dreams or something else.

I want to challenge you to a radical kind of death — *the Galatians 2:20 LIFE:*

"I have been crucified with Christ; it is no longer I who live, but Christ lives in me; and the life which I now live in the flesh I live by faith in the Son of God, who loved me and gave Himself for me."

In each trial you face, God may ask you to "die" to something that is not of Him, and be "resurrected" into the opposite which is freedom and life.

For example, when others attack you, you may find the Lord urging you to die to your need for man's approval, and to come alive in the knowledge that you are fully accepted and loved and even delighted in by the King of Kings.

Read Philippians 3:7-10. What is considered a loss in comparison with the surpassing greatness of knowing Jesus and following Him?

_____
_____

Jesus thought nothing of His stature as God when He crammed Himself into a mortal human body. He chose to die. What did He gain? See Philippians 2:1-18 and Hebrews 2:5-18.

_____
_____
_____

I hope you read those last two passages, because they're powerful!

What does Jesus call us in John 15:9-17?
_____

How did He demonstrate that He meant what He said? (See verse 13.)
_____
_____
_____

In light of that, what should your response be to the One who loves you like that?
_____
_____
_____

> "Then I heard a loud voice saying in heaven, 'Now salvation, and strength, and the kingdom of our God, and the power of His Christ have come, for the accuser of our brethren, who accused them before our God day and night, has been cast down. And they overcame him by the blood of the Lamb and by the word of their testimony, and they did not love their lives (so much as to shrink from) death. Therefore rejoice, O heavens, and you who dwell in them! Woe to the inhabitants of the earth and the sea! For the devil has come down to you, having great wrath, because he knows that he has a short time.'" Revelation 12:10-12

There is actually a special crown reserved in heaven for those who die for Christ's sake. It's called the "Crown of _____." (See Revelation 2:10 and James 1:12.)

This reward belongs to those who are faithful until death, who serve God well through suffering, who endure when tempted, who die to themselves, and who give their lives for His sake.

Will that crown be yours? Write a prayer of commitment to Christ based on each of those things in the paragraph above.

_____
_____
_____
_____
_____
_____
_____

Was that scary? Is there any form of persecution you're afraid of? Some way Satan or others might come against you that you think you might not be able to endure or overcome? Write a prayer handing those fears over to God.

_____
_____
_____
_____
_____
_____

Now ask Him what He says about that, and write what comes to mind.

_____
_____
_____
_____
_____
_____

What does Revelation 3:11 mean to your heart?
_____
_____
_____
_____

In heaven, we'll have no need of riches or power like so many people strive for here on this earth. So, what do we need a crown for there? (Revelation 4:10-11 might give you a clue.)

_____
_____

I don't know about you, but when I finally get to heaven and see Jesus face to face, *I want something of value to lay at His feet!*

Want to Truly Live?

Ask God to speak to you through 2 Corinthians 6:3-10, and write what you feel Him saying.

_____
_____
_____
_____
_____

What situations were those Christians faithful in?

v 4: _____
_____
_____
_____

v 5: _____
_____
_____
_____

v 6: _____
_____
_____
_____

v 7: _____
_____

v 8: _____
_____
_____

v 9: _____
_____

v 10: _____
_____
_____

Have you ever faced any of those? Highlight or circle them on the list.

In what ways have you personally faced persecution by people or the enemy for obeying Christ? Are you facing some kind of persecution now?

_____
_____
_____
_____
_____

Ask God how He wants you to walk through this trial. Write what comes to mind.

_____
_____
_____
_____

Is there something in you that is not of Him—some desire or need or sin or thought process or judgment that He wants you to die to that this trial is bringing up in you? Ask Him and write what comes to mind.

_____
_____
_____
_____

Now ask Him to replace that death in you with the opposite that is life (truth for lies, God's approval for man's approval, grace for judgment, selflessness for selfishness, etc.). Write your prayer here, and then purpose to walk out in freedom.

_____
_____
_____
_____
_____
_____
_____

Get in the habit now of daily dying to those things in you that are not of God so you can come ALIVE to the life-giving things of Christ.

Dare to Share Christ with the Lost

Hey! No Hoarding!

You have been given the most valuable gift of all time—salvation. You didn't do anything special to earn it. *Christ did it all.* (Ephesians 2:8-9; Matt 13:44-46; 1 John 3:1-3)

You carry within you the Treasure of Christ. (2 Corinthians 4:6-7) *But **He is not a treasure to be hoarded.***

What has Christ given you? Forgiveness. Heaven. Life. Freedom. Joy. Peace. Love. The list goes on. What jewels! Each is priceless. People in this world have killed to gain even just one of those! If you don't believe me, check out the news.

*Jesus is the answer to everything people are looking for. But **so many have yet to hear His name.***

Your dad and I grew up in two different countries, but both had many churches, and pretty much everyone had heard of Jesus.

The day we married, God called us to pastor an international church. Most of the attendees were unbelievers from closed countries where the gospel was not freely preached. They came to practice English, but also to find out Who this Jesus was their governments had hidden from them.

I still remember one man who interrupted my Bible study to ask what the numbers on the pages were (chapters and verses). And then he asked, "Who is Jay-sus?" pointing to His name.

Well, that was enough to propel your dad and me into a dark corner of the world where it's possible no one would hear unless we went!

Was it hard to leave our home countries? No, not really. Because *Jesus is our home.* **Wherever He is, that's where we want to be.** If He is headed into a turbulent country, calling us to a place where millions walk in darkness unless we bring in the Light, then we want to follow Him there.

When I get to heaven, I hope there's a throng of thousands who are there because I was faithful, because I loved, because I shared, because I didn't hoard my Treasure, but gave Him freely away.

Not that I shared with all those thousands. But I shared with this one, who shared with that one, who shared with ten, and poof! Thousands dancing at the foot of the throne!

I was hiking in the mountains of the closed country where we live and a local girl walked alongside me. I pointed to the mountains and asked, "Do you know who made those?"

"No," she answered. "They've just always been there."

I shared with her how God created the world and created her and loves her.

"If there's a God like that, then I want to know Him. I want to love Him back," she said. "But I think maybe my village must not be very important, because we've never heard this news before."

And yet, it is precisely because God loves her and her village so much that He arranged our meeting that day in the wilderness.

What if I'd stayed home in a comfortable chair reading a magazine? Well, actually, I *would* have if that's what God was doing with me that day. There's nothing wrong with relaxing. Jesus rested, too, when He lived on this earth. But *He also did whatever His Father led Him to do every moment.* And that's the point.

What is Matthew 28:19-20's Great Commission?
_____
_____
_____

Some argue that Jesus gave it to His disciples only, and it's not a command for us today. But I would argue that **anything in the Word that is the heart of God is most certainly a word for us today.**

How many people have not gone to the mission field because they don't feel "called"? *Perhaps our response should rather be, "I will go, Lord, unless You call me to stay!"*

Okay. That's my plug for missions. But don't feel guilty if you're one of the ones God calls to stay. Just, wherever you are, make the most of every opportunity to share His love. (Ephesians 5:15-16)

He has freely forgiven you; now forgive others. He has freely loved you; now love others. And as He has freely set you free from your sin, now share the good news with others so they too can be forgiven and go to heaven.

Don't let fear of what others think of you keep you from sharing Christ. **Remember that people are lost and headed for hell without Jesus.**

It's not about them liking you. *It's about Jesus, who loved them so much that He gave His life to save them.* So don't worry about how others respond. Just share. They are responsible for their response. You are responsible to **let Love rule you, not fear.** (1 John 4:16-18; Matthew 22:37-40)

Traveling alone to speak at a conference in South America, my assigned airplane seat landed me next to a burly soccer player from Argentina. As soon as that plane lifted off the ground, his face turned white as a sheet. He grabbed onto both armrests and rattled off a stream of Hail Marys.

I prayed silently, asking God for an open door to share about the perfect love that casts out fear.

Immediately the man looked over at me and said, "Why aren't you afraid?" Ding! Door open!

He was Catholic and religious, but had never heard the meat of the gospel. As I shared with him about Jesus, his hands eased their grip off the armrests, the color returned to his face, and before the plane landed, *Jesus had made His home in that muscle man's heart.*

Leading someone to Christ doesn't always happen that quickly, though. I have a best friend from high school I shared with for 25 years before she finally gave her heart to Him. In the end, it was our family's lifestyle of joy and love and fullness in Christ that spoke louder than words to her. She needed to walk together with us through both the good things and the bad to see His love in action.

Want to Be Useful?

Read Romans 10:13-15. What do you feel God saying to your heart through these verses?

_____
_____
_____

If you don't know how to share Christ with someone else, sign up for evangelism training at your church, or let someone show you some key verses to memorize (like the Roman Road), or find a good tract you can carry with you (like the Four Spiritual Laws or Peace with God).

Who do you know needs Christ? How will you share with them this week?

_____
_____
_____
_____
_____

Ask God to fill you with His Spirit and guide you to do whatever He wants you to do to draw those people to Himself.

Pray for the people you pass by this week. Look for opportunities to share. Ask God to speak through you and open their hearts to hear. Then dive in, trusting God to answer!

Get in the habit of looking for open doors to share Christ's love. Then walk through them without fear, asking the God who created each person and loves them beyond measure to speak through you in just the way that they will long for Him and accept Him with open arms.

Dare to Feed God's Sheep

20

Handing Out the Goods

Your great great grandmother—we called her "Mamoo"—fed a lot of hungry railroad workers at the turn of the twentieth century. She served them quite a feast: mashed potatoes and gravy, roast beef, biscuits, apple pie.... But she also served them a spiritual banquet of Jesus.

She never turned a "hobo" away, but always provided him with a meal, some work to do around the yard, and an earful of God's love.

She was a teenager when "Papoo" fell in love with her. But she' didn't want anything to do with his shenanigans in the saloons. Only after he accepted Christ and cleaned up his act would she marry him. Her faith and witness changed him forever. Even in his nineties, tears rolled down his cheeks whenever someone came to Christ.

On her deathbed in the hospital, Mamoo shared with all who would listen. She passed out so many Bibles, she continually begged for more.

I think it's the spontaneous moments of feeding God's sheep that awe me the most — when you find yourself telling some random story and being way too transparent to someone you don't know. Then the guy blurts out, "That's just what I'm struggling with! How did you know?"

What did Jesus say we would do if we love Him? See John 21:15-17. _____

All around you are hungry "sheep" only Jesus can satisfy. So hand them their True Pasture. (Jeremiah 50:7; Psalm 23) Don't shy away from teaching a Bible study or preaching if it's something God's asking you to do, even if you feel you'll be no good at it. *It's not about you anyway. It's about walking close to the One you love and **sharing that Treasure** with others who hunger for the "more."*

Let the name "Jesus" be the most common word in your vocabulary, whether others accept you for loving Him or not.

In fact, **leadership is a great way to draw nearer to Christ**, especially if you know you can't do it without Him. That time you spend at His feet as you prepare and listen for His leading will be some of your most powerful times with Him.

Here are some tips for Spirit-led sheep-feeding:

- **Pray as you prepare.** Ask God what He's doing, so you can speak what's on His heart.
- **Pray for the people** you will be meeting with.
- **Pray in the room** before the meeting. Get there 30 minutes early to ask God to fill the room with His presence.
- **Pray to start the meeting**, inviting God to do whatever He wants. Opening with worship invites God's felt presence, and helps everybody fix their eyes on Jesus, even before you dig into the Word. Don't worry if you're not musical. Some of my most incredible worship times have been with a music player and speakers. But make the words available.
- **Pray throughout the meeting**, even as you listen to others' questions or answers. Ask God to open their hearts and give you wisdom. Keep looking for what He's doing.
- **Pray afterward for God to seal in their hearts what He said to them**.

So, what's the key to feeding God's sheep through God's power, rather than your own? _ _ _ _ _ *

"Jesus said ... 'Do you truly love me?... Feed my sheep.'" John 21:15-17

Want to Make a Difference?

What did God teach you this week? Was there

a special scripture in your quiet times, or some circumstance or sermon that impacted you?

_____
_____
_____

Share that with others this week.

Ask God, "What opportunities do I have to feed Your sheep?" Is there a small group that needs a leader? Are there some friends that you want to study this book or some other Bible study together with? Is there an opportunity to lead worship? Is there a group of people He wants you to love or encourage? Write what comes to mind.

_____
_____
_____

Now hand that list back to Him and ask Him which of those He wants you to do. Then, as you step out in faith, *don't forget to pray and enjoy Him doing it for you!*

Get in the habit of sharing with others what Jesus is teaching you. Not only will it help you remember that truth and walk out in it, but most Christians are spiritually starved. They're not worshipping, reading the Word or listening to God on a regular basis. But if you're sharing some of your banquet food with them, they just might see how good He tastes, and head to His table for more.

Dare to Treat Women Right

21

Slippery Slopes

"No one will know if I look just this once. What harm can it do?" ... "She wants it. I'm just giving her what she wants." ... "I can't help it. I'm a man. I need it." ... "Everyone else is doing it, why can't I?"

What does James 1:13-15 say about the slippery slope of sin? _____ leads to _____ which leads to _____.

Temptation is normal. Every Christian faces it. (1 Corinthians 10:12-13) Don't fall into the trap of believing it's too hard to resist. Resisting the enemy's temptations is the very thing that makes him flee from you. (James 4:7) The more you resist, the easier it is to resist the next time. But the more you give in, the easier it is to give in, over and over, until you find yourself in a deep pit of captivity to that sin.

Jesus said if your mind even dwells on an inappropriate thought about a woman, you've already committed the act. (Matthew 5:27-28)

And Galatians 5:19-21 warns that impurity and sexual immorality will steal your spiritual inheritance from you. **That's a high price to pay for a moment of fleshly gratification.**

In 1 Timothy 5:1-2. How are you to treat older women? _____

Younger women? _____

All women? _____

What does Colossians 3:5-8 say about your actions and words regarding sexual matters?
_____
_____
_____

As you submit your thoughts to the Lord and align your desires with His, you will want to build hedges around yourself to keep temptation at bay.

For example, *choose to avert your eyes* from an inappropriate advertisement or scene in a movie. If your buddies are going out, *ask them where they're going before you decide* to go with them. If a woman who might spell danger for you is coming down the hall, *turn and go the other way*. If she calls you on the phone, tell her you're busy and *hang up*.

Purpose to stay away from alone situations with a girl, and to hang out together with other friends.

One time, your father and I were walking down the street to a restaurant in a country known for its sexual immorality. He tightened his grip around me and looked into my eyes.

I thought he was being romantic, but when we arrived at the restaurant, he explained to me that we had passed some scantily clad prostitutes, and he chose to look at the wife he loves instead.

At the pool the next day, several strikingly beautiful women lounged around topless. Your father turned his back to them, and focused on his precious treasures instead—his family.

He made conscious choices to keep his mind pure by where he placed his eyes and his thoughts.

With deteriorating moral values today and the influence of media, you may find yourself the only man in sight walking a pure road. But *walk it nonetheless*.

You are not yours to give away, *and neither is that daughter (or potential daughter) of the King you feel attracted to,* **until the day the King gives His consent and you are married**.
(1 Corinthians 6:12-20)

So **look at every woman as a sister of Christ**. Treat her with dignity, respect, and absolute purity, as Jesus would.

The woman God gives you for a wife will be a precious gift from Him. **Guard your kisses and your body as your wedding gift of purity and your vow of love to her** *and her alone as long as you both live. (She wants a Godly man too.)*

Want to Guard Your Treasure?

- What movies have you seen that portray women as objects to be used for sex? ***Ask God to clear your mind of those images, and to warn you in the future so you can refrain from watching such movies or scenes.***

- Is there a woman who might be "dangerous" for you? ***Ask God to help you build hedges of protection against temptation.***

- Are you tempted to look at pornographic images on the internet or in movies? ***Step away from your computer. Close your eyes. Worship God and read the Word. Fill your mind with the opposite of what the enemy wants to fill it with.***

- If you have a girlfriend, ***are you remaining pure in your thoughts and actions toward her? Are you building hedges to protect your heart, mind, and body from sinning against her (like keeping the door open and making sure others are around when you are together, not staying out too late or getting into situations where you will be tempted)?***

Is there anything you feel God moving you to repent of regarding sexual matters? Taks some time to do that. Write your prayer in your journal.

Then meditate on Psalm 73:25, and write a prayer to Him in your journal from that psalm.

Get in the habit of making sure others are with you whenever you are with a woman. If you find yourself alone with her, keep the door open, call a friend and ask him to come, invite her to go with you someplace public. Seek friendship with women, rather than an exclusive relationship that blocks out your friends, God, and any thought but her. Touch is a trigger that will drive you to want more, so guard yourself in that area. If you struggle, talk to God, remember He is watching you. Remember this is His precious daughter whom He loves and honors and is saving for her husband. Ask Him to help you overcome your weakness, to show you the "way of escape" every time you are tempted, and then follow Him there. (1 Corinthians 10:13)

Dare to Love Your Bride as Christ Loves His

22

Love that Lasts

Nearly all my friends from college are now divorced. What went wrong?

Well, *love did*, for one. I'm sure my girl-friends weren't perfect. Who is? But, the bottom line in every case was **the husbands were unfaithful.** Stupid. Stupid. *Stupid!*

In fact, one of my friends actually *forgave* her husband for cheating on her. But in the end, he wasn't willing to leave his lifestyle.

She married him because she loved him, but also because he loved God and wanted to spend the rest of his life helping people. So what happened to all that love?

Read Ephesians 5:22-33 and Genesis 2:23-24. What do these two passages have in common?

_____
_____

*Love is not an idea. It is not a feeling (although the feelings that accompany love are magnificent!). It is a commitment, a choice. And in marriage, it is a covenant—**a sacred, binding agreement for life.** In fact, it is so sacred and so binding that **the two become ONE.** (Genesis 2:23-24)*

This is not just a pretty phrase. *In the spiritual realm, the physical act of sex is a sealing together of two to become one.* **It is seriously binding!** You wouldn't chop your body up and throw away a piece, would you? *No!*

Read 1 Corinthians 6:12-20. What is your body meant for?

_____
_____
_____

What does that passage say sexual impurity is like in God's eyes?

_____
_____
_____

Now compare 1 Corinthians 6:12-20 with Ephesians 5:22-33. What do these two passages have in common?

_____
_____
_____

When you united with Christ, you became one with Him, and He became your "Head." In the same way, when you unite with your wife, you two will also become one, and you and Christ will be her "head."

Sex is the binding act within marriage that seals your covenant together. Can you feel the sacredness of that? It is also an incredible pleasure that will draw the two of you together in an intimacy unrivaled by any other experience on this earth!

If you give in to lust, or whatever else drives you to give your treasure away before you're married, God offers grace and forgiveness to a repentant heart, just as with any sin.

But, *this is something you really don't want to mess up!* Keeping your body sacred and set apart for your wife is one of the most precious treasures you and she will ever enjoy in this life! Not to mention there are serious spiritual ramifications for giving your body away outside of marriage, as you saw in the Corinthians passage we read.

That's why the enemy is already busy trying to turn your thoughts in impure directions. *Don't let him win!* (James 4:4-10) Those inappropriate relationships (even on the Internet!) outside of marriage can seal themselves upon your body and mind through visual memories and the accompanying "rush," causing serious trouble in both your spiritual and marital life.

Okay, so now we're back to the issue of love. Why do so many couples "fall out" of love?

To understand what love truly is, we must look to the One whose name is Love.

One of the main problems in relationships is that people use human ideas to define love. But no one on this earth can measure up to your ideal of love or anyone else's.

And that's on purpose, because *that need for love that drives you to look for it in so many places is meant to be fulfilled only by God. And He never falls short!*

You were made to love the Lord, opening a channel for His boundless love to flow through you to others in amounts you are otherwise incapable of. That means, *unless you are submitted to Christ, walking in a deep, intimate relationship with Him, you won't be able to love your wife as Christ.*

*The best leaders, the best husbands and fathers, are those who **follow Jesus well**. (Ephesians 5:23-24)*

As you lean on God and enjoy His endless love, then loving your wife with a selfless love will come naturally (5:25). Read the Bible with her and speak His truth into her life, so she will have the courage to walk in purity (5:26-27). Take care of her as a precious treasure (5:28-29). Be one with her (5:31) physically, spiritually, and in heart.

Listen to her opinions, her sorrows, and her difficulties. Pray with her and for her. When faced with a difficult decision, seek the Lord together. Study the Word and worship together. Have your separate quiet times, but also have a special time together with Him.

You may make mistakes, say hurtful things or make bad decisions sometimes. But just be quick to admit your messes to your wife and ask her forgiveness. (James 5:16; 1 John 1:9) Then seek God to help you repair whatever was torn apart.

Be one with Christ, and loving your wife with His love will come easily. (1 John 2:5-6)

Married to your father, I understand more what it means to be the bride of Christ. His love is tenacious, unbending. He has eyes only for me. He fights for me, stands up for what's right, speaks truth into my hopeless situations, and loves me through my messes.

When I was sick with a disease that left me in constant pain, he fought for me. He placed his hands on me and prayed, and each time he did, the pain subsided so I could rest. *That's when I understood the powerful authority a husband holds in the spiritual realm over his wife:*

If you speak blessings over your wife, she will be blessed. If you say ugly things to her, your words have power to curse. If you pray for her, heaven moves in reply.

Want a Love that Lasts?

What qualities of Christ's love do you feel you need more of in your life?

_____

_____

This is the time now to learn about true love. Ask God to highlight "love" scriptures. Mark them in your Bible as you come to them, and write them in your journal. You can even do a "Word Search" on the word "love," looking up in a concordance verses with that word in it. *Then practice living out what you see God's love is like.*

Stay intimate with Christ so His boundless love flows freely out of you. And keep your mind and body pure, both for Him and for the wife He has planned for you.

Get in the habit now of enjoying the limitless love of God and loving others well as an outpouring of His love He has already so freely given you. Then when you get married, loving your bride as Christ loves His will come naturally to you, and she will be the most blessed wife in the world.

Dare to Care About the Needs of Others

23

Empowered by Love

One day, as I hiked through the mountains of the closed country where we live, tired, thirsty and hungry, I saw an old woman resting by the road, her load of vegetables on the ground beside her.

Prompted by the Spirit (although anyone else might have thought lunacy), I offered to carry her burden. I hoisted the oversized load of squash onto my shoulders and we headed up a narrow mountain path to her village. Higher and higher we climbed. My back, unaccustomed to heavy labor, ached with every step, and I found it harder and harder to lift my legs. Inside, I cried out to God to strengthen me.

And He did. At last, a half hour later, after a climb that I'd spend a week recovering from, we arrived at the woman's home. She faced me, tears streaming down the crevices of her time-marked face. "I'm 83 years old, and no one has ever done anything like that before for me. Why did you do it?"

That day, for the first time in her hard life, she heard God's name, and saw His love in action.

"Bear one another's burdens." Galatians 6:2a

Jesus said every kindness shown to others is a kindness done unto Him. (Matthew 25:31-46) In fact, *the good things you do are evidence you are His.* (Ephesians 2:10)

Helping others is an act of worship.

In the middle ages, knights lived by a code of conduct called "chivalry." During a violent time in history, they were expected to not only be skilled at combat to defend king and kingdom, but also

- *to help the helpless*
- *to defend the weak*
- *to show courtesy to others*
- *to be gallant toward women*
- *to show loyalty to their king*
- *to be humble*
- *to serve God at all times*
- *to offer mercy to a vanquished enemy*
- *to live a life that brought honor to their king*
- _____
- _____
- _____

That's not unlike the code your King of Kings has asked you to live by as a man of God. Based on Micah 6:8, Isaiah 1:17, and any other scriptures that come to mind, check the things above He calls you to and add to the list anything else.

A man of God doesn't just look out for himself. (Philippians 2:4) He has a servant's heart that looks out for others. (Philippians 2:5-8)

If selfishness rules you, you will drown in it, never satisfied. But *if you love the Lord with all your heart and love others, serving them empowered by God's love, then you will find fulfillment and joy.* (Romans 13:11-14; Ephesians 4:2-3, 29-32)

Seek to understand more than to be understood, to love more than to be loved, to give more than to receive, to serve more than to be served.

As I was writing this chapter, a friend in need called from the hospital. I knew God was up to something. So, I hopped on my bike and rode the 45 minutes there.

Was it inconvenient? You bet! Your dad was on a trip and I needed to fix supper for you and your sister. The traffic was terrible. And it stormed lightning and thunder and torrents of rain—which I had to ride home in.

But God was magnificent! Not only did He minister through me (bringing her just the meal she craved, working out money details, finding her a caretaker), but the ride home was spectacular!

I breathed in the sweet, fresh fragrance of the rain that slapped my face as it vanquished the thirst of the drought-ridden land. And I worshipped. I called down His rains to fall upon the parched hearts of the lost people I passed.

If I hadn't fixed my eyes on God, though, I might have feared being struck by lightning or losing control on the slippery streets. I might have felt perturbed at the cold rain soaking me and stinging my eyes; or inconvenienced by the timing and the distance I had to travel.

I needed to look through His eyes at every turn not to miss the opportunity to love through the power of His love.

"And though I bestow all my goods to feed the poor... but have not love, it profits me nothing." 1 Corinthians 13:3

When love for the God who calls you to help others empowers you, and He is the one you meet as you worship Him with your life out there, ***then it is not a burden to carry your brother; it is exciting and wonderful.***

"Let all that you do be done in love." 1 Corinthians 16:14

Want to Look Like Jesus?

What are some practical things you can do this week to care for the needs of others? Ask God which of those He wants you to do and then obey.

_____
_____

Meditate on Philippians 2:1-18. Look back over the knight's code and your King's code for you. Write a prayer of fealty to the King of Kings to serve Him by looking out for the needs of others.

_____
_____
_____
_____
_____

Get in the habit of listening to others, caring about their feelings, and looking for ways to bless them or help them in time of need. Ask God questions like, "Lord, how can I bless my mother today?" or "What can I do to help that family or friend?" Then let Him lead you. When you have a servant's heart, you look a lot like Jesus. (Philippians 2)

Part V:
Improving Your Serve

Dare to Mentor and Be Mentored

Mentored See, Mentored Do

As a preschooler, you loved to copy me. If I leaned my elbow on the table, you would. If I spoke a sentence, you would say the same thing. Remember the fun we had?

What did Paul ask the believers he discipled to do in 1 Corinthians 4:16?

_____

Whom does Ephesians 5:1 say we should imitate?

_____

That's a pretty tall order, isn't it? Might be easier to stick to someone who's a bit more human, don't you think? Matthew 5:48 says,

"Be _____, therefore, as your heavenly _____ is _____."

It's one thing to play the copy game with Mom, and a totally different ball game to copy your heavenly Father!

So how is it that we're going to be so "perfect"? I mean, God Himself made us. Surely He knows we're flawed and prone to sin. Does the above command disturb you? Why or why not?

_____
_____

What does Hebrews 10:14 say to your heart?

_____
_____

This verse has become one of my life verses, because it totally sets me free to run with all my heart after God. For me, it means my mistakes have already been covered and I'm already "made" (past tense: it's already done!) perfect in God's eyes because of what Christ has done for me.

Now, the adventure is "being made" (present passive: it's in the process) holy—set apart to Him, pure, dedicated to Him. ***It's about relationship, not performance.***

1 Peter 1:16 is another "copy-me" verse:

"Be _____ because I am _____."

That sounds like a tall order, too. But what amazing God-thing do we get to set our hope on that takes the stress totally out of it and makes it all a joy? See 1 Peter 1:13-16.

_____
_____

God freely gives us His favor out of His bountiful heart of love, not because we deserve it, but simply because of what Christ has done for us. The result for us on the receiving end is unspeakable joy and gratefulness.

Okay. So now, the Word has set us up with the ultimate Mentor. He is the One we listen to and follow and imitate and run after. And ***our journey is Him.*** He is setting us apart more and more for His purposes to become more like Him as we fall deeper in love with Him. (2 Corinthians 3:17-18)

It's dangerous to become stagnant in your walk with God.

Think about it for a moment. What grows in stagnant pools? Bacteria and germs that make you sick. But *the stream that flows from the Source is clear, life giving, pure. It swells with the fullness of the Living Waters that flow into it, and flows across the land, transforming it into a place where plants grow, fish thrive, and people quench their thirst.* (Ezekial 47:1-12)

One of the most valuable keys to growing and "flowing" in the Lord all your life is to surround yourself with mature, godly people who have been through the hard things and come out victorious.

When someone close to Jesus shares with me a

difficulty he's gone through, I get to know God deeper through his trial. I can soak in the truth he teaches me that God taught him, letting it become a part of who I am as I walk out in it, even though I never went through the trial myself.

It's like what I overheard you tell your little sister when she was nine: "You can learn by listening to Mom and Dad's advice, or you can learn the hard way—by messing up. Either way you learn. But the first way's easiest."

Another good reason to have mentors in your life is **accountability**. They can *dig into the Word with you*, share their own experiences, *pray for you*, and *encourage you*; or *question your theology* if you're headed in the wrong direction spiritually. (2 Timothy 3:10-17)

They can also help to *hold you up in the face of temptation*. If you're tempted to misuse the Internet, for example, a good accountability partner might ask, "Have you been on the Internet this week? What did you do there?"

Paul encourages us to mentor others, as well:

> "The things that you have heard from me… commit these to faithful men who will be able to teach others also." 2 Timothy 2:2

If you love the Lord and are growing deeper with Him, then He is constantly showing you new wonders in His Word. (Hebrews 4:12-13; 2 Timothy 3:16-17) **What you have received from Him is not just for you, but also for the body of Christ.** (2 Corinthians 1:3-4)

So don't be afraid to mentor others. And don't worry about doing it "wrong." Different people mentor differently. I like to help believers walk in the Truth and go deep in the Lord. Can you tell?

My parents were my first mentors. They taught me about prayer, faith, love, truth and values that I will carry with me all my life. Another woman opened me up to deeper depths of God's love. Others taught me the power of worship and walking in the Spirit. Several more helped me tear down strongholds so I could help others do the same. And some amazing mothers helped me parent you wisely.

God has brought a string of incredible models into my life. *But my first model is Jesus.*

Anything someone else teaches me must match God's Word and His character, or I'm not going to imitate it.

Want to Grow Faster?

Who are some Christians you look up to? What are some godly things you see in their character?

_____
_____
_____

Ask God if any of these or someone else is a mentor He has planned for you.

Who are less mature believers you know? Are any of them hungry for God? Ask God to make it clear to both of you if He wants you to mentor someone.

_____
_____
_____

Mentoring can be done one-on-one, in a group, or just casually through hanging out with someone and speaking Jesus into his life through conversation and the way you live. Ask God to show you how He wants you to be mentored and to mentor.

Word of caution: *Don't mentor a woman one-on-one, unless she's your wife. Praying together with someone can be very intimate, and the enemy may want to use the feelings that rise up inside of you to tempt you to physical intimacy with the woman you pray with.*

Get in the habit of asking God what ways you need to look more like Him. Then look for believers around you who walk well in that. Ask them how they do that, and what journey they went through to get there. Surround yourself with people who look like Jesus, and you will find it easier to look like Him too.

Dare to Love

25

The Greatest Power on Earth

Have you ever met Christians who look down on others because they don't do this or that or don't do it right? Like "cookie cutters," they want every Christian to look alike.

But this life isn't about fitting into Joe Christian's box of dos and don'ts. What happens to people like that? See Isaiah 28:10-13.

_____

_____

_____

Kind of scary, huh? I'd rather walk in the freedom God gives me to be all He has made me to be, in my own uniqueness of loving Him and looking like Him, not Joe!

> "Love the Lord your God with all your heart, with all your soul, and with all your mind. This is the first and great commandment. And the second is like it: 'You shall love your neighbor as yourself.' On these two commandments hang all the Law and the Prophets."
> Matthew 22:37-40

So, reduced to one word, what is the only thing we're to be about? __ __ __ __

The two commands of that Matthew passage knock down every brick of the prison walls of legalism, because *it's not about how well you perform at this or that*, but…

Did you love? Did you love God? Did you love others? Then you have obeyed.

In tenth grade, one of my best friends was not a Christian. She loved to argue all her reasons why she shouldn't believe in God. Sometimes I just listened; sometimes I spoke truth. But I don't remember feeling defensive. I just loved her and longed for her to know Jesus.

When another girl started saying mean things to me, I said nice things back.

"Why do you do that?" asked my loyal lost friend, who respected me for my faith but couldn't understand it. I told her again of God's love. (Romans 12:9-21)

For years, she remained one of my closest friends ever. But it wasn't until she had children of her own that she had a change of heart toward Christ.

Her unbelieving home had been filled with strife, but my Christian home was filled with love. She wanted her children to grow up with a love like that and she knew from all our many conversations that Jesus was the reason for that love.

So one morning, she told God that if He was real, she would follow Him, but He would have to tell her how. Thousands of miles away, I felt the Lord prompting me to call her. And moments later, my friend I had loved for 25 years came to Jesus.

Now she has grown so fast in the Lord that she is one of my favorite people in this world to talk with about the deeper things of God.

Love changes lives.

Unfortunately, people have a tendency to create love boxes—ideas of what they think love is—and then try to fit themselves or others into them.

> *But if we love as God loves, we have a love without boundaries. We love, not because the person deserves it, but because He first loved us. (1 John 4:19-21) We forgive, not because what they did was okay, but because we have been forgiven.*
> *(Matthew 6:14-15)*

Likewise, because Kingdom Love doesn't fit in a box, it may look different in each situation. The same Jesus who rescued an adulteress and forgave her (John 8:3-11) also called the teachers of Scripture "snakes" (Matthew 23:33).

One seems more loving than the other does by human definition, but God knows each man's heart. A rebuke may be just what Love orders. (2 Timothy 4:2)

Love is surprising.

In one situation, God may ask you to love by helping someone. In another, He might ask you to love by letting him do it himself. Each person and situation and relationship is so unique, and His love is so wide and deep and long and high (Ephesians 4:14-19), that the realm of possibilities of what He might ask you to do out of love should not be limited to your understanding and expectations, but handed over to the Author of love who wrote a whole Book on it.

Love is forever.

God's love is an everlasting one, and one of unity. So as best you can, live at peace with others. Let them know you're willing to work things out, no matter how long it takes or how painful the process, and that you love them and accept them, even if they are different than you. (Ephesians 4:1-6)

Love accepts.

God is holy and perfect, and yet He accepts us and loves us just as we are at each stage along our journey, mistakes and all.

Love so deeply that others don't fear you as someone who angers easily and seeks retribution. (1 John 4:18) Rather, be someone who *fights for them and speaks God's words of love and truth to them.*

When I was thirteen, I began praying for the husband God would prepare for me. I didn't go to Him with a long list of looks or personality traits. I only asked Him for a husband who *loves Him first*, and *loves me second*. I knew that if I married a man of Love (1 John 4:16), we could make it through anything together.

Love overcomes.

Want to Beat Your Enemy?

What ways will you show God you love Him today?

_____
_____
_____
_____

Prayerfully read John 13:34-35, 15:12; Romans 12:9-18; and 1 Corinthians 13. Write down some things love does.

_____
_____
_____
_____

And things love does not.

_____
_____
_____
_____

In what ways have you been unloving?

_____
_____
_____

What ways do you feel Him leading you to show love to others today? This week? How is that a demonstration of His love?

_____
_____
_____
_____
_____
_____

Get in the habit of asking God how you can love those around you the way He loves them. Be willing to love even the unlovely. Let your love be freely given, not expecting anything in return, even as God has freely given you His love.

Dare to Forgive

Dangerous Decisions

Imagine a kite flying high and free upon the wind, no strings attached. **Now imagine the kite's string tied to the bars of a prison cell.**

Your heart was created to fly high and free in the joy and peace of knowing without a doubt the unending depths and heights of God's love.

But most people don't walk in that kind of freedom. Bound to lies that push them to fear, anger, and self-protection (John 8:42-47), they lash out at others, doing and saying hurtful things.

If you don't forgive them, it's like tying your heartstrings to their prison cell, letting their junk jerk you around.

You think about what they did to you. You imagine what you'll say next time you see them. You plot ways to avoid them. You imagine how to get back at them. Their offense plays over and over in your mind like a broken record, controlling your thoughts. *You need to cut the string and be free!*

What does Matthew 6:14-15 say happens to those who don't forgive? _____
_____

What does Ephesians 4:26-27 say happens if you let the sun go down on your anger? _____
_____

Did you know *most cases of depression and suicide can be traced back to unforgiveness?* If you don't forgive someone, even for a terrible offense that doesn't "deserve" forgiveness, your hurt and anger can turn to bitterness, then depression, which can result in either emotional or physical suicide.

Confronting someone on a sin is certainly in line (Matthew 18:15), especially when you do it in love. But don't wait for that person to ask forgiveness to forgive. *Just forgive.*

Unfortunately, offenders seldom admit to any wrong, even if you confront them. They go on about their lives like someone swinging his arms as he walks, never once acknowledging the black eyes that result from his carelessness.

You are the one who suffers when you don't forgive, not your offender.

Before we go further, it's important that you know what forgiveness is and is not.

- Forgiveness is not saying what that person did was okay. Sin is never okay.
- Forgiveness is not forgetting the action, although forgetting can happen if you forgive.
- Forgiveness is not letting them do the same ugly things to you and just "taking" it.

Forgiveness is releasing that person into the hands of God for Him to deal with, and releasing your own heart from the chains that bind you to the sin done against you.

God is your vindicator. (Isaiah 50:6-11) He is the One who judges each person's actions and deals with them accordingly, not you.

So, before you judge the other person for what he did, make sure the sin isn't actually your own.

Did you do something to instigate that person's response? Are you also in some way guilty of what you're accusing him of? Are you judging or mind reading (deciding what he's thinking or what motive he had)? (Matthew 7:1-5. James 4:10-12)

The best way to miss God setting you free is to point your finger at someone else.

In fact, you're likely to find yourself in the same kinds of painful situations over and over until you finally address the mess inside you and change.

I find about 80 percent of my pain comes from my own wrong thought processes. So, if I feel angry or hurt, I like to go to my divine Counselor and *ask Him why I feel that way*. I let Him show me any *related memories and lies* that might have entered my heart when those offenses happened (like "everyone's against me" or "I have to defend myself" or "I have rights, you know!") or any *vows* I might have made (like "I'll never let someone do that to me again!"). Then I **choose to forgive** those former offenders and **break those vows,** letting God's truth knock down my lies.

Usually, when I do that, the healing is so complete that the offense's sting disappears. But if that broken record tries to replay in my mind, I remind myself, "I forgive him. And I bless him in Jesus' name…" and I pray for him as the Lord leads.

Forgiveness is a decision. Even if you don't yet feel forgiveness in your heart, decide to forgive.

Satan wants a foothold of unforgiveness (Ephesians 4:26-27) so he can control you. But *don't let him.* Keep asking God what He wants to clean out of your heart until forgiveness is complete.

When you choose to forgive, bless, love, and pray for your offender (Romans 12:9-21), the enemy loses ground! Not only is your heart free from any stronghold of bitterness or hurt, but you have now begun praying for your brother's freedom as well. (2 Corinthians 10:3-5)

Forgiveness is dangerous to your enemy!

When you were about ten years old, some boys beat on you for no apparent reason. But you looked to Jesus, and felt Him showing you how their actions came from the messes in their hearts and asking you to love and forgive them. One of the boys was so humbled by your forgiveness that he apologized.

After the incident, we prayed together, in case any wounds had lodged in your heart. God showed us how the father of the boy who instigated the beating travels and is seldom there for him. Moved with compassion for him, you prayed for him and blessed him, asking God to mend the relationship with his father and set him free from anger.

Later, you sought ways to love him. You included him when others left him out. You even forgot about what happened! Eventually, he came to Christ. *Your loving forgiveness had eternal results!*

"If we walk in the light as He is in the light, we have fellowship with one another." 1 John 1:7a

Want a Light Heart?

Ask God, "Is there anyone I haven't forgiven?" Write what comes to mind.

_____
_____

Clean out your heart with Him, looking for sin and wrong thought processes. Are you judging? Acting vindictively? Write what He shows you.

_____
_____
_____

Choose to forgive. Remember, **forgiveness is a choice**, not a feeling. Each time the thought of what others did against you comes to mind, say, "I forgive (name), and I bless (name) in Jesus' name…" and then pray for them. **Lay down all your opinions of them at Jesus' feet, and ask Him how HE sees them.** Eventually, the hurtful thoughts won't plague you anymore, and **your feelings will match your choice.** Look for ways to demonstrate your forgiveness.

Be the bigger man. Don't let others' junk jerk you around. Grudges hurt you more than the person you hold a grudge against. So get in the habit now of immediately forgiving anyone who offends you. After all, you too have said or done hurtful things before, and God and others have forgiven you. So be willing to forgive quickly, even if others don't ask for forgiveness. Maybe, just maybe, your forgiveness will change them.

Dare to See with God's Eyes

Don't Judge by Appearances

1. Beware of that pretty face!

One of the greatest dangers you will face as a man is the lure of an attractive woman.

It's easy to believe you're in love with someone because of the rush you get when you're around her. But that rush may not be a godly one, even if she's a Christian.

If you are walking in intimacy with Christ, and submitting to His authority in your life, then you are most likely to discern correctly if a particular woman is the one He has for you.

But, my son, *do not be deceived.* Be on the alert in matters of the heart, because **your own heart may not be something you can trust.** (Jeremiah 17:9)

You could end up settling for less than the best, and even a mess, simply because your heart **yelled** *at you over God's* **whispered** *warning. (Proverbs 5)*

If this woman is godly and God has indeed prepared her to be the one for you, then **you will know it**, because *your callings and focus on Him—not just the rush in your heart or body—will align you together in Him.*

And I promise you, if she's the one for you, you will find her beautiful beyond measure, and your love together will surpass your every dream!

So, it's wise to talk with other believers you trust and spend a lot of time in prayer, listening to God's heart, *before* you make any big decisions in life, *especially this one.*

But again, remember that **even if you make a mistake, God's plan to draw you closer to Himself still stands.** So just keep walking toward Him.

There is forgiveness and grace, even through the consequences we face. But you want to choose the paths He has for you, not the paths you feel tugged down by an alluring woman.

2. Beware of first impressions!

Who did Samuel think should be king? See 1 Samuel 16:1-13. _____. Why?
_____
_____

Whom did God choose instead? _____

Man looks at the _____. God looks at the _____. (v 7)

In all things, don't lean on your own understanding (Proverbs 3:5-7; 1 Corinthians 8:1), but *ask God what He sees and join Him in His viewpoint.*

Not long ago, a cluster of villages in the dark country we live in was on my heart. I'd never been there before, and as far as I knew, neither had any other believers. Situated a bit off the beaten track, those villages would require an overnight stay. Not knowing anyone from there, I just left the whole matter in the Lord's hands.

One day, a couple of believers and I were on our way to a village in a different area to share Christ with a friend, and we stopped to eat lunch. As we prayed, a vivacious local teenager bounced into the restaurant and slammed herself down into a chair at our table, interrupting our Spirit-led prayer to chat about superfluous matters.

We didn't know her and she didn't know us, so such behavior was odd, not to mention annoying.

The whole thing seemed wrong on so many levels. After all, the Spirit was moving in our prayers and she stopped Him. In addition, she was rude and she talked all about herself. We were afraid we'd miss our bus, and she had interrupted our important God-led plans.

Everything inside me wanted to brush her off. Everything, that is, but Jesus.

He reminded me that He is in control, and rather than judge a situation by appearances, I should look for what He is doing.

As my heart softened to His touch and His voice, I began to really care about this girl and listen to her prattle. Not only was she hungry for the Lord, but *she was from the cluster of villages God had laid on my heart!*

Through her, He opened the door for us to go to her village *that very next week*, and **for the first time ever in that area, Jesus' name was heard.**

When this spunky teenager chose to follow Christ a few months later, He transformed her by the power of His love. No longer annoying or all about herself, she actually is now a doctor who spends her days caring for the sick "as if each one was my own mother or father." When medicine doesn't work, she prays for her patients, even though they've never heard of the God she prays to and don't understand what she's doing. When He heals them, she tells them about His love.

Fear of the Lord grips me even now as I write this story. I tremble at the thought of what might have happened if I had brushed her off based on first impressions. Her village would never have heard about Christ, she wouldn't know Him now, and neither would the others she's led to Him.

I'm so glad I surrendered my thoughts and opinions of that girl to the Lord so He could show me His and so we could follow Him down the exciting path He was leading us on!

3. **Beware of assumptions!**

You really don't know anyone like God does. So, imagining hidden meanings behind someone's words or actions is dangerous.

There is a real enemy who wants to divide and destroy, and he would love to make up quite a story in your head to turn you against your brother or sister. So, *don't assume you know what someone is thinking or meaning. Ask.*

According to James 4:11-12, are any of us equipped to judge others? Why or why not?

_____
_____
_____

There is only one Judge, and He didn't die and give us His job. So, be careful when you assume you know why someone did or said something, especially if you're assuming an evil motive.

Likewise, you don't really know all that's going on in that situation or how you should act in the middle of it. So…

Do not assess anything by experience or what you think you discern, but ask God how He sees it.

The best leaders I've had in this life are the ones that ask questions to find out what's going on, and then pray together with the people involved, seeking God's viewpoint and decisions on the matter.

But the leaders who make decisions based on their own imaginations or "expertise," rather than finding out the facts and seeking God's viewpoint, lose their best workers through foolish decisions.

So, whatever you face, take time to get alone with the Lord and **surrender your thoughts to Him, so you can take on the mind of Christ** on the matter.

I like to journal my thoughts to the Lord. I write out how I feel about something. Then I ask Him how He feels about it, and write whatever comes to mind, because usually that is His voice answering me. Then, as I read the Word, He is faithful to confirm His viewpoints and help me take on His thoughts.

For instance, when we had to move into a smaller apartment, I told God how I felt about it. Then I asked Him how He felt about it.

His voice answered in my mind, "I have a castle prepared for you." I laughed, thinking I must have heard Him wrong. But still, my heart was at rest, because I knew He would prepare the right place for us.

When the time came for us to move and the perfect apartment for our needs came open, lo and behold, the brass lock on the front door was in the shape of a castle!

We laughed so hard at God's humorous provision. Then, as an act of worship, we decorated our tiny apartment to remind us of the castle He's preparing for us in heaven.

After all, how big or how small our home here on earth is holds little importance compared to the eternal things a right-standing with God stocks up for us in heaven!

4. **Come up here!**

A few years ago, a close friend made some wrong judgments about me and cut off our friendship, unwilling to find out the truth or work things out. It was so painful because I had loved her with all my heart and was innocent of the things she accused me of.

But God was magnificent. He started doing a thing I call **"Come-Up-Here" moments**.

In my quiet times, He would pull me up to see from His eagle-eye perspective things I couldn't see standing in the middle of the situation with the mess all up in my face. (Ephesians 5:13-17)

Suddenly, my problems seemed so small. I *even found myself excited to go through trials, realizing they're a part of much greater things God is doing.*

Sometimes He would show me what He was doing in that friend, or in me, or even globally. But the air up high is sweet, and I know I can soar over anything with Him showing me how to fly.

Now, I don't want to see anything through my own eyes anymore. Just His.

"Stop judging by mere appearances, and make a right judgment." John 7:24 (NIV)

Want to See Clearly?

Are you struggling with an attraction to a woman who could hinder your walk with God? Ask God to give you purposeful ways to build a guard around your heart. Write what comes to mind.

_____
_____
_____

What other situation or people are you struggling with at this moment?

_____
_____
_____

Write out your opinions and ideas of that person or circumstance and lay them at Jesus' feet.

_____
_____
_____
_____
_____

Now worship God, and ask Him to show you His perspective. (Make sure you run what you feel Him saying through the Three-Fold Sieve in Chapter 8.) Write what He shows you.

_____
_____
_____
_____
_____

Get in the habit of looking through Jesus' eyes at every situation or person. Don't decide that your opinions and ideas are right, or that others are wrong. Just look for what GOD says. His opinion is the only TRUE one, and the only opinion that matters. As you look through His eyes, seeing what He sees, you will be able to walk out in His ways, leaning into what He wants to do, and what is yet to come by His power, rather than in what your human eyes call "reality." God, His purposes, and His kingdom are more REAL than anything temporary thing you can see or touch on this earth.

Dare to Submit to Authority

28

Blessing Those Above You

I once had a boss who, almost daily, dictated what I could and could not wear. He paid the female employees less than the male; and his unqualified friends were promoted over me, even though I had experience and tenure.

Often he fabricated stories, and then barged into my office to angrily accuse me of them. When I'd smile and listen, he would fume all more, "Why don't you cry or get mad?"

When he found out God was calling us overseas, he terminated my job early and cheated me out of more than $1000.

Was it easy submitting to that man? No. In fact, to keep my heart in the right place, I had to write on a piece of paper in bold letters, **"I don't work for him; I work for God,"** and tape it where I'd see it every day. God gave me the strength and wisdom I needed in each circumstance, and I not only made it through, but also grew.

Not all bosses are like that. But the truth is, in this life, you may often find it much easier to submit to God than to submit to the human He has placed in authority over you.

Think about it. You please God just by being His son! But some earthly authorities are impossible to please. What if your boss, teacher, or parent is irrational, demanding, controlling, or vindictive? What if he asks you to do things you can't possibly do? What if he asks you to do something immoral?

How does God want us to act toward our leaders? See Titus 3:1-2. _____

Why? See Hebrews 13:17. _____

What is to be our attitude toward governing authorities and police? See 1 Peter 2:13-17. Why?
_____
_____
_____

How does 1 Thessalonians 5:12-13 say we should treat those in authority over us?
_____
_____
_____

That's a lot of verses on submitting to authority, isn't it? And we haven't scratched the surface yet.

God is perfect and holy, and yet He places imperfect people in leadership positions over us and then asks us to obey them. Why?

1. **To testify of His greatness.** (Daniel 1:17-21)

In the story of Joseph, each time he was wronged and his position was knocked down to the worst degree, he worked for those above him as unto the Lord. God blessed him, and he gained favor and was able to share with unbelievers about God.

What about Daniel and his friends? In what ways did they glorify God under the pagan king who captured them and dragged them from their homeland? See Daniel 1:17-21.
_____
_____
_____

Daniel excelled in his work and was given a chance to testify to the king about God. How did the king respond? See Daniel 2.
_____
_____

2. **To grow.** (2 Corinthians 12:7-10)

Each time my boss did something unjust or made my job more difficult, I had a choice: to be angry and bitter, or to lean on the Lord and do what He was doing. When I chose the latter, I grew stronger in my walk with Him.

But the best scenario for growing, of course, is working with godly authority.

The editor at my first writing job marked up my work with myriads of red scribbles. But I learned and grew under his correction.

When I began doing women's ministry, my leader modeled a lifestyle of worship and surrender. She taught me to let Jesus be the one to lead my Bible studies. When I did something wrong, she told me why it was wrong, so I could learn and grow.

But growing isn't always so easy. I have a friend who was hurt once by a boss who didn't support him. When he joined a new team, he felt compelled to do things behind his new leader's back, rallying others to join him. At last, he realized this leader loved him and was for him. He asked forgiveness, and received the blessing of a godly covering as he served the Lord under a man who was for him and God's purposes.

Submit to your leaders, be a joy not a burden, pray for them, respect them, love them, live in peace with them, and honor them.

Whatever you do, do it as unto the Lord.
(1 Corinthians 10:31-33; Ephesians 6:5-8)

Remember He will strengthen you (Philippians 4:13). So no matter what job you do, keep your conversation running with Him. Let Him guide you through each difficult circumstance, flood you with His peace (Philippians 4:5-7), and make even the hard things turn out for His good (Romans 8:28).

But what if your leader forbids you from doing something God has asked you to do? What did Shadrach, Meshach, and Abednego do? Daniel 3.

Sometimes standing up for the Lord in your job can be costly. We have friends who served God as leaders in a Christian organization for nearly 20 years, but when edicts came down from above, which were contrary to the Word but which they were required to enforce, they resigned. All those years down the drain? No. *They obeyed the Lord, and **obeying the Lord is never a waste!*** (Deuteronomy 28:13)

Your father and I work in a country where Christians are often arrested and beaten for their faith. We know at any moment that we could be ripped from our home as Daniel was. (Daniel 6) But will we stop worshipping God and living for Him, sharing His love with others? Not likely!

So if a day comes that you, like Daniel, must stand up and say to someone in authority over you, "I will not bow to your idols," then do so with love, bringing glory to God. (Daniel 6)

Want to Succeed God's Way?

What authority figures are in your life right now (parents, teachers, employers, government leaders, etc.)?

Pray for them and write down some ways you can bless some of them this week.

Ask God to prepare for you just the job He has for you. Even now, get in the habit of submitting to your leaders and being a blessing to them. If you honor those in authority over you and do all your work as unto the Lord, He will bless you, just as He did Joseph.

Dare to Walk in Integrity

29

Living from the Inside Out

Are you the same person when others are watching as you are when no one else is around?

Seeking to understand the intricacies of driving in the country where we live, your father asked a taxi driver, "Can you turn right on red here?"

"Sometimes," he answered.

"What does that mean, 'sometimes?'"

"Well, if a policeman's there, you can't. But if he's not, you can."

Funny huh? ... But what do you think?

It's past midnight, no cars are coming. Do you run that red light? Do you slide through that stop sign?

Do you watch that movie when no one knows you are? Look at that magazine? Go to certain sites on your computer? Watch that sexy TV show? Masturbate?

That's a tough one. After all, who's to know? You're not hurting anyone when there's no one around to be hurt, right?

Integrity begins on the inside.

What does Ephesians 5:1-18 say about hiding sin?

_____
_____
_____

What does God's light do to it?

_____

What are you to be filled with that is so different from the rest of the world? (v 18)

_____

What does Luke 11:33-36 say to your heart?

_____
_____

In light of that Scripture, how might watching a sex scene in a movie affect your relationship with Christ and your testimony to others, even if no one knows you watched it?

_____
_____
_____

What you do in the dark is not hidden from the spiritual realm. The more you entertain dangerous thoughts, the easier it becomes to give in to them. And once you've given in, even just once, the easier it is to be trapped and imprisoned by the enemy in that area of your life. *It's sin's slippery slope.* (James 1:14-16)

The truth is whatever you hide in secret the enemy can use against you. So, if you are entangled in a secret sin or thoughts that could lead you to sin, it's a good idea to share with one of your mentors or someone you can trust who will pray with you and help you through to freedom before it gets any worse.

Okay, now that we've established that a man of God lives from the inside out (that inside being filled with the Holy Spirit), let's look on the outside.

Integrity speaks of a man's reputation, especially regarding honesty and high moral values.

For example, a man of integrity:
- *doesn't lie.* (Colossians 3:9)
- *seeks out the truth and speaks it boldly.*
- *keeps his promises.*
- *doesn't steal, cheat or engage in secret thoughts or deeds of darkness.* (Ephesians 5:11-21)
- *doesn't slander, but speaks good things behind*

others' backs. (Romans 12:9-21) He is a man others feel they can trust or confide in.

- *is known for his love for God.*
- *has the reputation of living God's Word, not just reading it. (James 1:22; Galatians 2:20)*
- *fears God, rather than man. (Galatians 1:10)*

A man of integrity doesn't let the persuasive words of others move him to do something contrary to his convictions, but he unwaveringly stands on the Word and on the solid Rock of Christ as his model. (Ephesians 5:1. 1 John 4:19)

> "'Teacher,' they said, 'we know you are a man of integrity and that you teach the way of God in accordance with the truth. You aren't swayed by men, because you pay no attention to who they are.'" Matthew 22:16b (NIV)

Your father is a man of integrity. Many times, I've watched him stand his ground and do what God and the Word tell him to, even in the face of opposition.

One time, some friends of ours tried to get us to break the speed limit. They had so many "good" reasons. But for your father, your sitting in the back seat was reason enough not to. He didn't want to model for his son that breaking the law is okay. (1 Peter 2:13-17)

> "Encourage the young men to be self-controlled. In everything set them an example by doing what is good. In your teaching show integrity, seriousness, and soundness of speech that cannot be condemned, so that those who oppose you may be ashamed because they have nothing bad to say about us."
> Titus 2:6-8 (NIV)

I feel so honored to be married to a man who lets the Word guide his actions, rather than the persuasive arguments of men. (Romans 13:1-3)

Men of integrity often have the best marriages, are the best fathers, get the best jobs, find the most fulfillment in life…

But the greatest reward you will enjoy as a man of integrity is God's presence. (Exodus 33:11-17)

> "I know that you are pleased with me, for my enemy does not triumph over me. In my integrity, you uphold me and set me in your presence forever." Psalm 41:11-12 (NIV)

Want to Stand Straight?

The Word is full of instructions on how to live a life of integrity before God and man. Each one is a jewel that brings freedom and purpose to your life. (Psalm 119:17-22)

Check out the following verses and write what these men of integrity were characterized by:

Proverbs 10:9: _____
Proverbs 11:3: _____
Proverbs 13:6: _____
Psalm 25:21: _____
Psalm 78:70-72: _____
1 Kings 9:1-5: _____
Nehemiah 7:2: _____
Psalm 7: _____

Pray and ask God to show you any "secrets" that are making you stumble. Write a prayer of release from these, cutting off the enemy's rights to attack you in those areas, and surrendering your thoughts to God. (2 Corinthians 10:3-5)

_____
_____
_____
_____
_____
_____

> Get in the habit of baring your heart before God. He already knows all your secrets, so it doesn't do you any good to "hide" anything from Him. Instead, let Him show you how to let go of the things that mar you, so you can grab hold of the things that build you. You want to be known as someone others can trust, a faithful friend and husband, who does the right thing. (1 Peter 4:15-19)

Dare to Glorify God in Everything

The Highest Honor

In ninth grade, a burly Korean boy threw a fastball, and the first baseman ducked. That's what you do when Big Kim throws the ball: *you get out of the way.* But I missed that advice somehow, and caught it in my face!

As I sprawled out on the grass, the top half of my vision in blackness, my friend DJ's face appeared in the bottom half, just beyond a tuft of grass, grinning in fascination. "Look! Her nose is on the other side of her face!" she exclaimed excitedly. (DJ is now a doctor, by the way.)

Kim felt so bad about what happened that he came to my house nearly every day to check on me. My face was swollen up like a blue puffer fish, and I had difficulty breathing, so I wasn't up to visitors. But I sent him messages through my father. I wanted Kim to know I forgave him and Jesus loves him.

Repeatedly, Kim asked, "How can she forgive me after what I've done?" Repeatedly, my father shared with him about God's love and the difference He makes in people's lives.

After a couple of weeks, and some talented plastic surgery to put my nose back where it belonged, Kim showed up at my house once again, this time with a tiny gold cross he had brought as a gift for me. Tears in his eyes, he said, "I decided to follow Jesus, and I wanted you to be the first to know."

I still have that gold cross today. It's a mark of God's glory I will never forget.

You know, come to think of it, my Jesus got beat up, too, so that I might be saved. I wonder if I looked a bit like Him during those black and blue days. (Matthew 27:30)

Hopefully, you won't ever get your nose or anything else busted up, but spiritually speaking, **the more you look like Jesus, the more glory you bring Him.** (Philippians 3:7-11) It's what you were created for. (Isaiah 43:7)

He has set you on a pilgrimage to know Him ever deeper, and to make Him known ever louder, as He transforms you into His likeness, with ever-increasing glory. (2 Corinthians 3:12-18)

The more you love—love God and love others—the more you will look like Him and bring Him glory. (Matthew 22:37-40)

Let the things you do every day be the things that turn eyes God's way!

You're going to make mistakes. Everyone does. But even your sins and flaws can point people to the Lord. The act of saying, "I was wrong; please forgive me" to someone you've hurt SPARKLES with His glory. (1 John 1)

So don't be afraid of your mistakes. Make them an opportunity to bless others.

Yes, *bless!* People don't like it when you pretend you're perfect. They'd rather see you real: sharing your troubles with them, admitting when you're wrong, and serving the Lord because it comes from your heart, not to put on a show.

It's possible that one day people will know of you because of something you've done in this life. But my prayer is that it will be something *He* has done, not you, and that *no one will be able to mistake that.* (Psalm 115:1)

Do only the things God asks of you.

Once you prove yourself a faithful follower of Christ, many people may ask you to do this or that. They might even use guilt or manipulation. But worrying about what others think of you can lead to burnout.

Burnout happens when you do more than God asks, or you do it in your own power.

So, please don't go there! You are too precious a laborer in His fields to frazzle and take a nosedive.

Even if people get angry at you, **do only what God asks you to**, and then **lean on His strength to do it**, not your own. (Colossians 1:28-29; II Corinthians 12:9-10; Philippians 4:13)

Leave plenty of time in your schedule to be alone with the Lord.

One of my mentors used to say, "If on any given day, there is no room in your schedule to spend 1-4 hours with the Lord, then there's something wrong with your schedule."

She has a point. If you don't spend time with the Lord, how will you know Him? It's like marrying your wife, and then ignoring her.

You might even want to schedule personal retreats with the Lord in addition to your quiet times, where you can steal away with Him for a whole day, or even several days.

Remember, you were made for relationship. If you make glorifying Him about what you *do*, rather than about *being one with Him*, you will miss the whole point.

Make the most of every opportunity.
(Ephesians 5:18)

I hopped in a taxi one day for a ten-minute ride to the bus station in the closed country where we live. Within seconds, the driver began confessing sin to me. I didn't know the language well at that time, so in my "baby talk," I asked him, "Would you like to wash your heart?"

"Yes!" he screamed. "How can I?"

I told him God loves him and sent His Son to die for him so his sins could be forgiven and he could have eternal life. Right there, in five minutes of hearing about God's love, that man gave his heart to Christ.

I handed him a Bible in his language that I happened to have in my bag (God had planned this encounter from the start), and as I hurried off to catch my bus, he yelled after me, clutching his new treasure to his chest, "I can't wait to tell my wife!"

A lot can happen in ten minutes.

"Therefore, my beloved brethren, be steadfast, immovable, always abounding in the work of the Lord, knowing that your labor is not in vain in the Lord." 1 Corinthians 15:58

Want to Shine?

What opportunities to give God glory are in your path right now?

_____
_____
_____
_____
_____

Hand those things over to Him to make sure it is what He is asking you to do. Then seek Him to do it through you, for you, and even, perhaps, in spite of you. (2 Corinthians 12:9-10)

Write John 3:30 into your own prayer to God.

_____
_____
_____
_____
_____

Get in the habit of seeking to bring glory to God every moment of every day. Walk close with Him, asking what He's doing and listening for His answers, so you walk in step with Him (Galatians 5:25), and others will see His light in you. And shine, every moment, every day. Let Him be your Light, as you light the way for others.

"Whatever you do, do all to the glory of God." 1 Corinthians 10:31b

Is God leading you to gather several young men to study these life lessons from the Word together? Then, first, a prayer of blessing for you:

"Father, thank you for Your servant who has chosen to make a difference in the lives of these young men. Pour out Your anointing and Your blessing, and unleash Your power to flow in mighty measures as they gather to meet with You. Open the doors of each heart, and then rage in like a mighty flood. Invade their space, get up in their face, and speak so loudly that none can deny You are near. On Your servant who is leading, I ask for an extra measure of wisdom, sensitivity to Your leading, surrender to You, and empowering to walk out in this challenge each week. When we feel weak, Lord, make us strong. May our teaching not be with persuasive words, but with Your power, so that all eyes are turned to You." (1 Corinthians 2:4-5, 13; Deuteronomy 32:2; 2 Corinthians 12:9-10; Colossians 1:28-29)

I suggest you assign 1-2 devotions a week to these young men because of busy schedules and time needed to digest and walk out in the lessons they are learning. Working through each of the lessons as a group, rather than in personal quiet times, also works well. The schedule you decide on will depend on how many weeks are available to you to study together and what you feel the Lord leading you to do.

As young men sign up to come, advise them to bring their Bibles, this book, and a journal to the meetings. Encourage them to write in their journals every day, noting what God is teaching them in their quiet times and through life experiences. You keep one, too. It's an excellent way to commit God's words and lessons to memory and to life.

The smaller the group, the easier it is for everyone to participate. So, generally, groups of 4-8 make for the best discussions. But let the Lord lead you in this. You don't want to cut anyone out He might be leading to join, or drop the opportunity just because only two want to study.

Mothers or fathers may also use this book with their sons, and include their daughters as well, as these truths come from Scripture and are for all believers.

Everyone has different leadership styles. Feel free to ask God how HE would want to lead these sessions. But, for your information, here are some keys He's taught me:

- **Be accountable.**

    If you don't already have a mentor (see Chapter 21), pray and ask God about whom you can ask to cover you as you lead. This could be a pastor or staff member of your church, or just a godly friend. You need someone who will pray for you through questions and difficulties.

    In addition to mentors, I often have a "right-hand man" with me when I lead small groups—someone who will come early and pray with me in the room, then sit with us praying and participating throughout the meeting, then debrief with me afterward. If I get sick or can't lead for some reason, this person can step in for me. This can be another adult, or it can be one of the young men in your group.

- **Enlist intercessors.**

    Get the parents and other intercessors involved in praying for you and these young men as you study and meet each week. But keep private things said in your meetings confidential.

- **Stay ahead.**

    Do these lessons in your quiet times, but don't wait until the day before you lead. Study them early so you have several days or a week or more to walk out in the truth yourself before you teach it. The richness of your own experience will motivate those you lead to have their own deep walk with the Lord.

- **Pray.**

    Follow the prayer guideline in Chapter 20.

The more you pray and surrender these studies and these young men into God's hands, the more powerfully He will move.

- **Begin with worship.**

I suggest about 20-30 minutes of worship, as the Spirit leads, at the beginning of each meeting.

Give freedom to everyone to worship any way they feel comfortable. Some may sing, some may lift their hands, some may sit still, some may lie down, some may kneel, some may draw, and some may even sleep! Don't let anyone judge another for the way he worships, but let everyone feel comfortable.

You might want to intersperse spontaneous Scripture reading or prayer throughout the music or invite people to express verbally how great God is or read a psalm—however the Spirit leads.

Afterward, you might want to ask what they felt God saying during the worship time, before you move into the lesson study. This will encourage all of you to look for what God might be doing.

You can lead the worship time yourself, or enlist someone else to lead worship each week. It's wonderful to have live worship with instruments and such, and some of the young men in your group may play instruments and be willing to help in this. But audio worship music from a music player you can hook into speakers is also an excellent option.

I suggest you ask the boys which worship songs touch their hearts. Then keep a list (including the songs you enjoy Him with) to draw from to arrange worship.

I also like to assign young people to look for God in the secular songs they listen to. Most love songs speak of a love beyond human ability, even though they're written about humans. The only One who loves like that is God. Everyone on this earth has a deep-seeded need for God's love, and many end up writing songs about it, even unknowingly! But I don't suggest you use secular songs to worship to as a norm. Even if they point to Him, they are not as rich as the music He has led His body to create, anointed for such a time as this.

How do you arrange a worship set?

For 30 minutes of worship, you're usually looking at about 6 songs.

Make sure you have the words to those songs available for each person present so everyone can participate to the fullest.

Organizer-types might begin with praise songs about how wonderful God is, and follow with more intimate songs, such as about how much He loves us and we love Him. Or you can do it the other way around, too. But my favorite way to arrange a worship set is to pray, then listen to God. Whatever songs pop into my mind after dedicating that time to Him, I begin arranging how they feel like He's leading. I'll usually make sure the end of one song flows easily with the beginning of the next song.

The best way to know how to lead others in worship is to worship in your own quiet times. It's never a waste of time to surf through worship songs on the Internet and look for ones that touch your heart.

- **Expect God to show up.**

Be looking for God during the sessions, so you can follow whichever direction He's leading. Don't worry if you don't cover the lesson or if you need to meet together again to discuss the same theme.

It's not about getting something done; it's about *drawing closer to Christ*. Just let the Holy Spirit have full freedom to lead you in His directions. Most definitely plan for each session, but listen to God as you plan, and surrender the meetings over to His leadership.

- **Pray for each other.**

   Whenever someone shares from his heart or mentions something he feels God leading him to do, stop everything, gather around him, pray for him, and encourage him, reading any Scripture appropriate to the situation. This teaches the young men to minister to each other. Encourage them to call each other during the week to ask about each other and pray for each other.

- **Be transparent.**

   Be real with these young men, so they will feel free to be real with you. Share about mistakes you've made and how God grew you through them. If you don't understand something in the study and aren't sure how to walk out in it, feel free to say so, and ask the boys to pray for you during your time together that week. Then be prepared to share the next week how God answered, or how you are still working on it.

   You are also free to write morethanaconquerorbooks@gmail.com to dialogue with the author about questions.

- **Keep confidentiality.**

   Whatever is shared in each session should stay within the group so that each person feels safe. If Joe tells a story, no one can tell it outside the meeting, unless Joe gives his permission.

   Another key to helping the young men feel safe is to have a closed-door policy. Only those who are committed to come are allowed to come. No newcomers once the group has been established.

   But this needs to be discussed and prayed about together as a group. If, after the doors are closed, someone wishes to join, you should ask God about it together, because that person may be sent there by Him. So be flexible according to His leading.

- **The Word is your source.**

   If someone asks a question, don't just answer it. Make it an adventure to dig into the Word for the answer.

   If someone asks, "Is it okay to smoke?" for example, don't just say "No" or "Yes." Look up Scriptures in a concordance that deal with our bodies or glorifying God, and assign the boys to prayerfully read those scriptures during the week, asking the Lord to speak to them. Then come together the next week to see what God said. Or, read the scriptures there in the meeting together, praying and asking God to speak. This teaches them to go to God for the answers to all of life's questions.

- **Encourage discussion.**

   As you prepare, ask God to give you some good questions to ask from the lesson, or scriptures for the boys to discuss.

   Some people are more talkative than others are, so listen to the Lord as to how to draw the quiet ones out and rein the vocal ones in. You want everyone to participate, as He's doing different things in different people, and we all need each other to grow together in Him. (Ephesians 4)

Here are some ideas for discussion questions:

- What was this chapter about? Summarize in your own words.

- What did you like about this chapter? Why?

- What did you not like? Why?

- What touched you the most about this chapter? What did you feel God speaking to your heart?

- Is there anything God is asking you to do? A command to follow? A sin to confess?

- How do you plan to walk out in that?
- How are you doing with walking out in what we talked about last week?

- **Give the participants opportunities to lead.**

The ones who lead are usually the ones who grow the most (that means you, too!), so ask God to direct you in assigning leadership tasks to different ones in your group to lead in prayer or worship or even in some of the sessions. Have them take turns in these different tasks, so each one has a chance to develop and grow in different areas of leadership,

Check out these

More than a Conqueror Books

*"We're not just about books; we're about books
that make a difference in the lives of those you care about."*

www.morethanaconquerorbooks.com

morethanaconquerorbooks@gmail.com

Delight to Become a Woman of God
30 Devotionals from a Mother's Heart to Her Daughter's on Drawing Near to Christ and Loving Well

Do you have a sister or a friend that might benefit from a daily devotional like the one you just read? *Delight to Become a Woman of God* is filled with Scripture, drawings, and thought-provoking questions to teach young women to walk out in who they are as the bride of Christ, and to live and love through Christ's love. (Group study leader's guide included.)

Rescue from the Kingdom of Darkness
Book 1: *Chronicles of the Kingdom of Light*

Snatched from their summer fun by a sudden tragedy, six friends loyal to the King of Light embark upon an unforgettable adventure into the Kingdom of Darkness to rescue a young boy held hostage by evil creatures. Astride such mystical mounts as a winged tiger, a flying unicorn, and a giant cobra, these ordinary young people engage in an extraordinary battle that will cost them more than they counted on. As they struggle against monsters—and even each other—to overcome the fight against night, the friends soon discover the true enemy that must be conquered is the enemy within themselves.

This first book in the *Chronicles of the Kingdom of Light* draws young people deeper in their relationship with Christ, learning how to listen to His voice, know the Truth of who they are in Him, and stand against the enemy in life's daily battles.

Sands of Surrender
Book 2: *Chronicles of the Kingdom of Light*

Banished by the King of Light, Cory cannot continue the search for his kidnapped brother until he discovers a way back into the Kingdom of Darkness. When creatures of Darkness offer to lead him there, he agrees to follow, a decision that costs him his freedom and exposes a plot against his family so dangerous he may not make it out alive. Meanwhile, Victoria sets out on her own misadventure, placing those she loves in such terrible peril, Cory's life is not the only one she must save.

This second book in the *Chronicles of the Kingdom of Light* uses humor and adventure to teach young people truths that open the door to freedom from strongholds, so they can walk in the intimacy with the King of Kings they were created for.

Made in the USA
Lexington, KY
16 October 2016